Britain and 1940

The year 1940 was the most significant in European history during the last century. Its reverberations are still with us. But the implications of what happened in 1940 have meant different things in different countries. For Britain it was 'the finest hour', the beginning of a People's War. How did people foresee 1940 before it happened? How were representations changed over the years? What does 1940 mean now?

This book covers the prehistory of 1940 in Britain, tracing the great fear that a second world war would perhaps mean the end of British civilization. It charts the development in wartime culture and popular politics of the myths of Dunkirk, the Battle of Britain and the Blitz. It describes the varied ways in which the myths of 1940 have impacted on British politics and attitudes to the outside world since. Malcolm Smith argues that myths are historical events in their own right, that they form conceptions of the past, that they need explanation rather than exposure as 'lies'. The book presents a panorama of the influences that have constructed national consciousness around a crucial moment in British history.

Malcolm Smith is Senior Lecturer and Chair of History at the University of Wales, Lampeter. He teaches in the field of war studies and British popular culture and his previous publications include *British Politics, Society and the State*.

Britain and 1940

History, myth
and popular memory

Malcolm Smith

London and New York

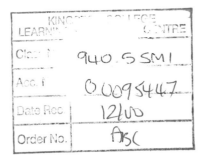
First published 2000
by Routledge
11 New Fetter Lane, London EC4P 4EE

Simultaneously published in the USA and Canada
by Routledge
29 West 35th Street, New York, NY 10001

Routledge is an imprint of the Taylor & Francis Group

© 2000 Malcolm Smith

Typeset in Times by BC Typesetting, Bristol
Printed and bound in Great Britain by
Biddles Ltd, Guildford and King's Lynn

British Library Cataloguing in Publication Data
A catalogue record for this book is available from the British Library

Library of Congress Cataloging in Publication Data
Smith, Malcolm, 1947–
    Britain and 1940: history, myth, and popular memory/Malcolm Smith.
        p.   cm.
    Includes bibliographical references and index.
    ISBN 0–415–01050–0 (hard cover) – ISBN 0–415–24076–X (pbk.)
    1. Great Britain–History–George VI, 1936–1952. 2. World War,
    1939–1945–Campaigns–Western Front. 3. World War, 1939–1945–
    Great Britain. I. Title.

  DA587.S65   2000
  941.084–dc21   00-059139

ISBN 0–415–01050–0 (hbk)
ISBN 0–415–24076–X (pbk)

Contents

Figures

Acknowledgements

I would like to thank my colleagues in the Department of History at Lampeter for their friendly encouragement over the years. Thanks also to the Library staffs at Lampeter and the National Library of Wales, Aberystwyth. Thanks above all to Deborah and the boys – I hope they find something interesting in what follows.

New Quay, February 2000

1 Introduction

This is not so much a history book as a book *about* history. It dwells in particular on the relationship between academic history and popular memory – by which I mean the things that people implicitly believe rather than what historians tell them. Broadly, I have three aims: the first is to describe the pre-war myth of 1940 – what people expected the next war to be like; the second is to deal with the construction of the myth/s of 1940 during the war itself; the third aim is to trace the changing construction of what 1940 and the war have come to mean in the subsequent sixty years.

The third of these aims has been a peculiar experience for me to work upon. It led me to understand that I was writing a history of my own times and, quite literally, reconstructing my life. Those of us of a certain age have probably become aware over the past decade or so, as we have celebrated the fiftieth anniversaries of the start, the course and the end of the Second World War, that we have become for younger people the object of historical curiosity in our own right. We are all walking historical texts in some sense. There is a personal motivation for writing this book: there always is in every book, of course, but it is not always made explicit. Those of us whose parents fought the Second World War have never got over the realization, normally at age nineteen, that at exactly the same age so-and-so's father had been flying a bomber over Berlin, or taking a tank across the Rhine, or painting stones white in Catterick. The war permeated our lives, even though we never saw a bomber or heard a siren. The photographs in the family album still haunt us, even if those photographs may be fading. What the war meant to those who have been born since is part of the legacy of that war, and in itself deserves understanding and analysis.

In what follows I do not intend to debunk the experience of 1940. It seems to me to have been the one genuinely heroic moment in twentieth-century British history. Britain was fighting alone against something which simply had to be stopped if any kind of acceptable values were to survive in Europe. What interests me is what happened to 1940, culturally, and what the British came to think about that experience. I use the word 'myth' here to signify not a load of lies to be uncovered, in the way that historians often use the word – particularly, in this instance, Clive Ponting in *1940: Myth and Reality*.[1] Many readers find a book which works constantly at the theoretical level somewhat tedious, so I have decided to state my theoretical perspective here and not to repeat it at length in the course of the book. I realize that in so doing I run the risk of criticism that I am not working on a consistent enough intellectual framework but, on balance, I accept that risk in the hope of greater accessibility.

I am using the word 'myth' to mean a widely held view of the past which has helped to shape and to explain the present. More often that not, I will be using the term as a collective noun to suggest the collection of smaller myths that make up the larger story of 1940; there is a myth of Dunkirk, a myth of the Battle of Britain and a myth of the Blitz, among others, but they are unified in the mythic structure of 1940 as a whole. Seen from the perspective of the social sciences, it does not matter whether myths approximate the reality of the past, whatever 'reality' may mean anyway in a postmodern age. What does matter is that these myths are implicitly believed and that they help people to make sense of their lives, that they offer a popular memory which explains the past and the present and moulds expectations of the future. A social group or a nation becomes a social group or a nation only when it has a common mythology, and a common sense of the past is a very significant element in the collective identity of any interpretive community.

It is a larger part of that 'imagination' which Benedict Anderson wrote about in defining nationality as an 'imagined community'.[2] Lévi-Strauss posed the question: 'When does mythology end and history begin?' His answer was that mythology is essentially static: it works for a given moment in time but, as new problems refuse to sit easily in the mythological framework, so a new mythology must develop if the grouping is to retain its coherence.[3] In this line of thinking, history may be seen as the succession of mythological structures, each of which works for its own moment in time; and each generation's, social grouping's or nation's sense of the past is a mythological structure which will be superseded. If we add to Lévi-Strauss' notion of the relationship between myth and history a Gramscian perspective on the way in which dominant groups in a society adapt and negotiate successions of hegemonic compromises, we come a fair way to suggesting what is involved ideologically in mythological change, and in whatever is historically dominant at any given moment.[4] The views of Michel Foucault, on the all-pervasiveness of power, on the construction of normality and of deviance in the interstices of language and all other modes of representation, constitute for me the intellectual foundation of this study.[5]

The ways in which this process works are, clearly, complicated. Professional historians would still generally like to see their role as guardians of the past, or even as the police-force of the popular memory. It cannot be said that they have been very successful in that role. History may remain a major academic discipline in Britain, but it does not have the intellectual clout it had forty years ago. This is partly due to the proliferation of '-ologies' over this period, which claim a greater 'scientific' basis to their truth than the truth of historians. But it is also due to the fuller development of a more serious and responsible attitude to retelling the past on the part of broadcasters and film-makers, who have at their disposal the 'irrefutable' visual 'truth'. These people may be more serious and responsible than their predecessors, but they do not share the methodology or even the aims of academic history. Historical advisers working on 'factual' television or film projects are not normally the most respected members of the team. Most forms of popular culture, and in particular those visual forms which now dominate, cannot deal very effectively with the nuances, the debates, the uncertainties that pepper academic discourse, the 'ifs' and the 'maybes' of history, as Natalie Zemon Davies put it.[6]

In Britain as in America, though much less so in France and Italy, the visual documentary has inherited from literature the realist narrative tradition, which seeks, as Roland Barthes put it, to disguise the artificiality of its production.[7] It presents itself as a sort of mirror, and therefore as 'real'. Academic history is too finicky for this style of popular culture; for the film-maker, historians undermine their own authority by their refusal to be certain about things, and film-makers in turn have no way of conveying these uncertainties adequately. Moreover, the production values of television documentary series such as *The Great War*, *The World at War* or *The People's Century* clearly overwhelm. They manage to combine solemnity with mesmeric visual footage to produce a truth-claim, which no historian working in traditional media could hope to emulate. In turn, feature films such as *The Dam Busters*, *The Battle of Britain*, and *Schindler's List* borrow such techniques to make their own equally seductive truth-claim. Most people learn much of their history from popular culture, and specifically from the mass media. This is something that historians are learning to live with, but also to investigate, as historians such as Robert Rosenstone and others are in fact doing.[8] I hope that this book contributes something to that investigation.

While popular culture may control perceptions of the 'big facts' in history – the wars, the kings and queens, the genocides and the revolutions – academic historians perhaps can control the 'little facts', even if only because the general public is not all that interested. It is probably also the case that it is academic historians gnawing away at the 'little facts', the nuanced interpretations, the finickiness, which produces those periodic paradigm shifts that change the 'big facts'. The year 1940 is my case in point. 'Dunkirk', 'the Blitz', 'Winston': these are not just neutral terms, they are totemic. They are the 'big facts' of 1940. They are, I will later argue, largely based on visual images, the films of Humphrey Jennings and others, the photography. It is because they are visual, because they rely on the claim that 'seeing is believing' that they become very difficult to reinterpret. These visual images have become the essential shorthand by which the meaning of the war has been conveyed, in thousands of newspaper, magazine and televisual references. They carry with them enormously powerful discourses on British national identity, rooted into the popular memory of the war, embodying all the associations of phrases like 'finest hours', 'backs to the wall', 'community spirit', 'people's war'. The very fact that one need do no more than set these phrases down, without any need to explain them, suggests what one means by the mythic quality of 1940, and in itself testifies to the enormous success of the myth. Such phrases are the captions by which the visual images are translated into language, thus borrowing the truth that seeing implies.

For the generation of the 1950s and 1960s in Britain, the 'big fact' was that 1940 was still the turning point of British history, when the prejudices of the Victorian and Edwardian era, still felt to hold sway in the 'locust years' of the 1920s and 1930s (again representation is controlled largely by visual imagery), were swilled away in a new spirit of national consensus. A caring state replaced an uncaring state as the war against fascism produced a war for the New Jerusalem of the welfare state and Keynesian economics. It was not just the change in political direction which Britain took – a change confirmed by the Labour landslide of 1945 – that was deemed important. Something more sublime than mere political change was involved. The year 1940 elicits high-sounding rhetoric even from the most staid writers. At the end of his long and still academically respectable account of Britain between the wars, first published in 1955, Charles Mowat concluded: 'In the summer of 1940, as they awaited the

Battle of Britain, they [the British people] found themselves again, after twenty years of indecision. They turned away from past regrets and faced the future unafraid'.[9] Mowat's history was framed by mythology. In his and other historians' formulations, 'interwar' gave way to 'contemporary', the 'bad times' gave way to the 'good times'. At this remove, Mowat sounds a little glib: to suggest that the British were not a trifle worried about the prospect of the Luftwaffe is surely gilding the lily. But the point Mowat implied was that 1940 was much more than a change of government and a military crisis; it was a high point of national consciousness. A young mother, interviewed by Mass Observation as early as VE Day, when asked what she remembered about 1940, replied, 'I was happier then, daring myself not to tremble as the bombs fell, when I got romantic letters from abroad, when I cried about Dunkirk. When people showed their best sides and we felt we were fighting to gain something'.[10] If 1940 could be seen as a high point of national consciousness, the full impact seems soon to have dissipated into a nostalgic glow in the popular memory. That nostalgic glow is still with us in Britain, backlighting contemporary history, since representations of 1940 still constitute the foundation myth of a new Britain seen to have emerged from the war.

Not that Mowat's version of events has gone unchallenged. Historians have challenged the 'big facts' with little ones, a cumulative and attritional attack, from different directions, though without as yet wholly undermining the big picture. Angus Calder in *The People's War* in the late 1960s attacked from the left the opportunities missed, as he saw it, in not capitalizing on the spirit of 1940. In his view, and those of others on the Left in the 1960s, 1945 was the modern equivalent of 1660, a restoration of traditional values.[11] Tom Harrisson, in *Living Through the Blitz*, went back to the Mass Observation archive he had amassed during the war and declared himself amazed at the way 1940 has been sanitized and given heroic status in the years since.[12] In the 1980s, Corelli Barnett focused the New Right's attack on the supposed sublimity of 'the finest hours' in *The Audit of War*.[13] The point is that these books, in challenging the historical orthodoxy of the 1950s and 1960s, are attempts to restructure the sense of the past and thus, albeit indirectly but not wholly unconsciously, attempts to restructure the present. History, by which I mean not the past itself – which is simply dead and gone and cannot be reconstructed – but the way in which historians interpret the past, has been changing substantially to accommodate new problems which sit uncomfortably in the static framework of the original myths. In what follows I will be centrally concerned not so much with what 'really happened' in 1940 as with the construction of what happened, the process of the production of the myths themselves, before 1940 and in 1940, and also with the myths' changing significance since, in which historians have played their part. Mythology has its own history, and it matters what people believe happened in the past, no matter how they learned it. Myths, in other words, are not there simply to be debunked in the name of historical accuracy; they are important historical events in their own right, and they are central to the common sense and to the history (which is part of the 'common sense') of the period in which they hold sway.

One particular example of debunking is particularly germane to this book. Angus Calder, who did so much in the late 1960s to challenge the cosily patriotic view of the home front during the Second World War, returned to the subject in the early 1990s with *The Myth of the Blitz*.[14] Second time around, Calder was writing in the aftermath of the Falklands War, when one particular aspect of the myth of 1940 had been mobilized to project Margaret Thatcher as a resurrection of Winston Churchill, leading a Britain doggedly fighting alone again against a foreign dictator. Calder's anger over what he saw as the abuse of 'Churchillism' during the war in the South Atlantic is the mainspring of the book. It is a work which deals effectively and imaginatively with the status of 1940 in the imagination of a nation which had thrown out traditional labourism, in the 1979 general election, and with it whatever remained of what had been thought of as 'the postwar consensus'. In spite of Calder's protestations to the contrary, he does often fall into the trap of attempting to deconstruct the myths counter-factually. In the case of Dunkirk, for instance, he makes extensive use of Nicholas Harman's debunking 1981 book, *Dunkirk: The Necessary Myth*. In Harman's view, the retreat was a British collapse, not a result of Belgian or French ineptitude, and the British Expeditionary Force fell back to the coast more often than not as a disorderly mob. If British soldiers were scared of capture by the SS after the murder of 170 British prisoners, they should have blamed their fears on the Durham Light Infantry, who had already murdered perhaps 400 SS POWs. Operation Dynamo itself involved the 'methodical deception' of the French who were tricked into providing cover for the evacuation by their perfidious allies.[15]

'Facts are stubborn things', as John Cornford put it, but facts do not speak for themselves. They make sense only when they are selected and put into a story. Harman wrote his book because he believed that, after all this time, the British could stand the 'truth'. Calder clearly felt the same. But the 'truth' is that putting such material into the public domain seems to have hardly altered anyone's view about Dunkirk and the events that preceded it. The point about Dunkirk is that its 'little facts' can be obliterated by the larger story about 1940 as a whole. In 1940, the book *Guilty Men* could blame the defeat in France on the weaknesses of British leadership in the 1930s. The escape of the army, even without its heavy weapons, gave Britain the chance to start again under a new national leadership, and the rot was stopped, firstly by 'the few' in the ensuing Battle of Britain, and secondly by 'the many' in the Blitz – and then the torch was handed back to the Army to carry at Alamein and D-Day. The 'People's War' overcame not only fascism but also the near treachery of the élite of the 1930s, which had brought Britain so low in May and June 1940. The exposure of counter-factual details misses the point that the metanarrative surrounding Britain's rebirth in 1940 explains such exposures as simply 'details', explicable and redeemable given the larger, more positive story.

I am simplifying Calder's book enormously, however, to suggest that it is simply counter-factual. He accepts that myths are, as it were, bigger than facts. He accepts too that myth-making was essential in such unprecedented circumstances, and that its implications were not all bad: the myth 'was firmly oriented against snobbery, selfishness and greed and could be given a forthrightly egalitarian emphasis'.[16] Rather more contentious is his claim that 'by the time war broke out in September 1939 the myth had been all but scripted'.[17] There are indeed similarities between some images of the nation before the war and those that came to dominate in 1940 and beyond, but the similarities are largely superficial. What is central to the myth of 1940 was that the present and the future were both radically different from the past. In fact, as we shall see, the imaging of 1940 was itself a site of quiet ideological struggle, not at all a foregone conclusion, and a struggle that was never quite resolved. The myth was never simply one-dimensional. There were not just nuances but also straightforward internal contradictions in the story, and these contradictions have themselves played important roles in the history and the development of the myth in the years since.

The year 1940 raised questions about Britain as an imagined community – questions about the relations between the governors and the governed, between the regions and the centres, between the social classes, between the sexes, between the recent past and the future in political, social and cultural terms. It also raised major questions about Britain's external image, how she viewed herself and felt herself to be viewed in relation to the rest of the world. The fact that Britain survived to fight another day in 1940, seen from the narrowly British perspective of the myth, disguises the worldwide and long-term implications of the overall German victory in the West. As David Reynolds has argued, 1940 need not have happened in the way it did. Given the relative strength of the German and Anglo–French forces, there could quite easily have been a rerun of the Western front between 1914 and 1918. Crucially, however, 1940 was not a rerun of the Schlieffen Plan. Over a few weeks, Germany altered the balance of power in Europe in a way that she had not been able to do in four years in the Great War. The consequences made that year 'the fulcrum of the twentieth century' not just for Europe but also for the world.[18]

Consider what might have happened had the Manstein Plan broken down in 1940. Rubbing shoulders with the French for years in a second titanic conflict with Germany in Western Europe may well have persuaded Britain that her traditional policy towards Europe was no longer viable. The outbreak of war in 1939 was clear evidence that British policy since Versailles was wrong-headed. Already by early 1940, the Foreign Office was touting the radically new idea that a strong Anglo–French coalition was the only permanent counterweight to Germany in the West after the war. It is legitimate to speculate that such a view might well have become widespread had it not been for what happened in May and June 1940, and that Britain might well have committed herself firmly to European ties in 1945. As it was, Britain survived 1940, and her leader went on to become one of the Big Three dominating the direction of the war and the shape of postwar Europe. Largely, the British considered that 1940 and what followed meant that she should continue in her stance as an offshore island, no longer bestriding the world herself but hanging on to the coattails of a nation which did.

For the rest of the world, the defeat of France was a great deal more significant than Britain's subsequent survival. This does not mean that the rest of the world was right and Britain wrong; it means that the rest of the world constructed a different 'truth' of 1940, using the same set of facts but in a different context; but for Britain, there were two 'truths' about 1940. Churchillian rhetoric and standing alone against the dictators created an international myth of continued great power status, to co-exist with the myth of the people's war at home. Churchillism was clearly at work in domestic reactions to the Suez crisis in 1956, and to the Falklands and the Gulf and Kosovo crises in later years. It remains a most potent factor in attitudes towards European integration, European football and even in the contemporary heritage industry.

For many Scots, Welsh and Irish, on the other hand, it is simply an excuse for unwarranted English nationalism. For many English, too, it is the embarrassing downside of living in an old country. In short, the myth of 1940 and its contradictions continue to permeate British lives. It contributed to the birth of a new Britain after the war, a country with a welfare state which not even the Thatcher revolution could eradicate but, paradoxically, it also contributed to the Thatcher revolution itself. Why else would the Spitting Image puppet of Margaret Thatcher wear a siren suit and carry a big cigar? Events have clearly moved on. The structure of assumptions that underpinned 'postwar' have made way as the end of not just a century but also of a millennium approached. Tony Blair convinced middle England to vote for him in 1997 not by restating the priorities of parliamentary socialism victorious in 1945 and central to the mainstream left in the 1960s and 1970s, but by adopting the stance of Thatcherism with a human face. In the war over Kosovo, the *Guardian*'s cartoonists clothed Blair not in the Churchillian siren suit but in the string of pearls and dress of the Iron Lady. The year 1940 and its aftermath have passed into 'proper history' and no longer command the here and now as they did until the 1970s. As a result, it is now easier to judge 1940's impact in shaping postwar Britain.

2 The projection of war, 1918 to 1939

It is a truism to say that Britain was not prepared for the Second World War. Little effort had been put into preparing the Army for its role in 1940. The extent to which the British Expeditionary Force was to suffer for that is a measure of the degree to which Britain had become obsessed with the threat of air attack since 1918. However, it is easy to underestimate just how much had been achieved. 'Preparation', after all, is a relative term, and it can be shown that German preparation also had many crucial weaknesses; in no sense did Germany outgun the West in 1940 in the Battle of France. The fact is that continental commitment had not been the top priority for Britain between the wars. By 1939, Britain was actually spending more than she had ever spent on armaments in peacetime. She had introduced conscription without any of the hand wringing that had accompanied the introduction of the first such measure just twenty-three years previously. She had begun to organize her aircraft industry in a way that was to contribute substantially to survival in the Battle of Britain. Spitfires and Hurricanes were not conjured out of a hat by the Churchill government in the summer of 1940; they were the product of long-term planning. Britain had also organized a large-scale programme of civil defence, designed to cope with a wholly new method of attack which threatened the massive destruction of industrial and dormitory areas of Britain – with gas, incendiary and high explosive. This was necessary as the next war, it was confidently predicted, would be very different from the last, because this time the people themselves would be the targets. The myth of the 'next war' dominated interwar assumptions, and framed preparations for a conflict which, if it could not be avoided, was deemed virtually certain to be even more apocalyptic than the last.

If the introduction of air war meant that the experience of the Great War was not much to go on in preparing for the next, there were still some vital lessons to be learned, particularly in the area of organization and planning by the state. Total war, as the years 1914 to 1918 had proved, was above all a test of the state as an institution. Economic potential was of no use if it were not mobilized by a central planning authority. People would not go on fighting for a government in which they had no confidence, or which deliberately repressed them without explaining the national need in acceptable terms. The lessons of Russia in 1917 and Germany in 1918 were all too clear in that respect. Liberal ideology had been placed under severe threat as a consequence in Britain. Slow but steady increases in intervention by the state had been essential to carry the war to a successful conclusion. The Ministry of Munitions, for example, spent £2000 million during the war and, by 1918, employed 65,000 staff.

Even though British institutions proved flexible enough to take the strain of the war, there had been signs of incipient unrest among workers, in the Shop-Stewards' Movement on Red Clydeside for example. This was accompanied by a significant political shift at the top. Lloyd George had been unable to keep the Labour Party in the wartime coalition. While Lloyd George and the Conservatives between them were able to hold Labour at bay in the huge victory for the rest of the coalition in 1918, Labour had clearly emerged at last as a major electoral force, prompting a change of front on the part of the other two major political parties. Within a few years, the Liberals – who had been in power either in their own right or in coalition continuously from 1906 to 1918 – had ceased to be serious contenders for government. The strains of running the war, and the electoral breakthrough for Labour, overwhelmed them. Thus a major political force of the nineteenth century appeared to have evaporated simply because of the war.

Although revolutionary forces had been held in check with relative ease in Britain, the point was that total war had produced changes which could neither be foreseen nor fully contained. This was not just a crisis for liberalism. The concessions which government was forced to make to maintain the war effort meant that the relationship between the social classes had drastically changed. War had simply become too dangerous for conservative forces to contemplate with any kind of equanimity. Although the depression which followed weakened the wartime power of the trade union movement, there was to be a continual fear in the ensuing years that the effortless domination of the nation by the aristocratic–bourgeois alliance, which had lasted since the end of Chartism, was up for grabs.

What price victory? Three-quarters of a million British had died for gallant little Belgium and for the destruction of Prussian militarism. True, the British Empire was bigger than ever, with the League of Nations mandates given to Britain after the war, but widening the Empire had never been a public reason for going to war and was as much a burden as an asset, as Palestine was to show. In Europe, the situation facing the victors was unprecedented and very dangerous. After the great continental war of a century before, the major powers had at least emerged intact, if weakened politically by the ideas of the French Revolution. This time, the collapse of the monarchies of Russia, Austria-Hungary and Germany left Central and Eastern Europe in a monstrous tangle of ideologies and nationalities. The Romanovs and the Habsburgs may have been tyrannies as far as Liberal Britons were concerned, but they had at least given some sort of shape and predictability to their massive domains. The only certainty about those regions in the postwar years was that they were very unpredictable.

When the Bolsheviks finally emerged as the victors in the Russian civil war, their country was so devastated by the conflicts since 1914 that it would be years before the Soviet Union could exert any real influence in European affairs. When the Soviet Union did begin to exert influence, social democrats could only assume that it would be of an even more insidious kind than that of the old Russian Empire. Austria-Hungary collapsed into a series of successor states, none of which looked strong enough to provide a new stability in the area. The great paradox was that, in defeat, Germany was actually in a stronger position *vis-à-vis* Eastern Europe than she had been in 1914. She would be difficult to stop if she decided to cut loose again, even if there was the political will to do so.

Just as importantly, Germany did not believe she had been defeated. There had been no Waterloo this time. Germany had sued for an armistice in 1918, but she had certainly not surrendered. By the time the allies were ready to serve their terms, the situation in Germany had deteriorated to the point where she could do nothing but accept them, but this cut no ice with those right-wingers who believed that Germany had been sold out by the 'November criminals'. Nascent social democracy in Germany had to carry the burden of the peace terms, which may have crippled Weimar from the start. But by the end of the 1920s, social democrats looked capable of beating off the challenge from the political extremes, and were also beginning to win sizeable concessions from the allies, at Locarno and over reparations.

Then the depression hit, fatally undermining Weimar and shifting power to the Far Right.

The prehistory of 1940 was founded on the interplay of domestic worries in the wake of the Great War, with deep uncertainty about the future of the international structure which had been so thoroughly destabilized by the conflict. In the best of circumstances, it is perfectly understandable that the most destructive war in history should produce deep-seated anti-war sentiments. When those sentiments were combined with fears over continued political control by the national elite, compounded by a long-lived depression which at times threatened to institutionalize the preconditions for social revolution, the nervousness of government preparation for a second Great War becomes even more explicable. The spectre of communism was haunting Europe, spawning its polar opposite in fascism. That ideological conflict threatened to sideline social democracy entirely.

In constructing some sort of logic out of this matrix of problems, the British appeasement of Germany was an obvious, indeed virtually unavoidable answer. The size of the German population and the scale of her economic potential meant that she could not be held down indefinitely without force. Either Germany resumed her role as a major power right in the centre of Europe, her grievances appeased and her aggression curbed thereby, or stability would never return to the continent. Without political stability in Europe, there would never be economic stability. As long as there was economic instability, there was the chance of revolution from either Left or Right, and there were soon countries in Europe to serve as models for either revolution.

So appeasement was a perfectly rational ambition, even if it was not exactly heroic. With hindsight, we can see that it was almost certainly doomed to failure from the start. Too much had been changed, but too much was also left in precarious balance to be easily reordered. It is not part of my argument here to justify the policies of the 1930s, merely to point out why it was that Britain had to find 'guilty men', once the policies of the interwar years had failed. What would happen in a future war had shaped perceptions of the future, and framed actions in the 1930s. Interwar politicians followed the lines they did because they were dominated by priorities quite different from those which dominated in 1940. Baldwin and Chamberlain reigned over a broad consensus in the 1930s, as the two general elections of the decade seemed to show. Saving the economy, the mainspring of government policy through much of the 1930s, was seen as the most hopeful way of saving social democracy and providing a platform for the stabilization of Europe. The year 1940 exchanged one mythology for another.

A set of hopes replaced a set of fears, and the fears were dismissed as the simple weakness of a group which had led Britain astray.

Between the wars, it was the bomber which became the prime signifier of the grim future. In 1917, 150 people were killed and Liverpool Street station was destroyed in the first major raid by German bombers on Britain. Thus ended nearly nine hundred years of immunity of the British people from foreign attack, give or take the occasional coastal raid. The Channel had been bridged, and the Royal Navy was no longer Britain's guaranteed defence, or so it seemed. The impact of this first strategic air attack was immense, coming as it did on top of growing evidence of the significance of aircraft in the tactical sphere on the Western front. By the end of the war, the Royal Air Force (RAF) had been formed as the world's first independent air service, its primary mission to develop the means to project strategic bombing deep behind enemy lines, with the aim of undermining the German economic structure and the political will to war. The argument for independent air power had much force in the circumstances. Lloyd George himself was reputedly scared stiff by air raids during the Great War (and was again seen 'very white and greatly excited' after the false air raid warning on 3 September 1939).[1]

It was argued that the confusion and panic caused more generally by these first raids was out of all proportion to the number of bombers which actually attacked. If, as seemed clear, no breakthrough was achievable by land forces in France, given the enormous strength of defensive positions and the enormous resources that modern nations could use to shore up a defensive position, then it seemed logical to literally leap over the trench deadlock and to attack directly those targets behind the lines – the factories, the workers who made the guns, the politicians who directed the war efforts – without whom the war could not continue. If war had continued into 1919, General Sir Hugh Trenchard would have launched a major strategic air attack on Germany with a force of long-range bombers grouped specifically for that purpose, the Independent Air Force, the forerunner of Bomber Command.[2]

In fact, the RAF spent much of the first decade of the interwar years fighting for its very existence as an independent force. The Army and the Navy wanted their air arms back, both of which had been incorporated into the new force. With no clear enemy in sight in the 1920s, it was not at all clear what was the point of maintaining such an inherently aggressive weapon as the long-range bomber. Air Chief Marshal Trenchard, as he had now become, argued persuasively that the successful use of the RAF in imperial policing missions demonstrated the overwhelming psychological effect of air power. It achieved its effect by the sense of powerlessness it engendered in its victims as much as through physical destruction. It was also, a point at which politicians pricked up their ears, demonstrably much cheaper as well as less costly in lives than the traditional army punitive column. Air power was to be projected by many of its champions in this period as a strategic stiletto, aimed at the heart of the enemy, much more economical than the heavy club provided by land forces or the slow strangulation provided by sea power. The defeat of Russia in 1917 and of Germany in 1918 seemed to demonstrate that the key to victory now lay not in defeating the enemy armed forces but in defeating the enemy nation. The bomber offered a way to achieve this by attacking directly the inherently vulnerable economic, political and social targets behind the front lines.

The problem was that Britain was more vulnerable than most other nations to the effect of such attack. The bridging of the Channel by aircraft meant that London could be paralysed by a sudden knock-out blow. By the beginning of the 1930s, London was just fifteen minutes' flying time from the Channel coast, too close for any effective defence to be organized, it seems. The bombers might even appear entirely unannounced by flying up the Thames estuary. Paris and Berlin, by contrast, could only be reached by arduous deep-penetration raids into French or German air space. For the RAF, the vulnerability of Britain, and London in particular, made it essential that Britain accept a One Power Standard in the air, either to deter aggression or to act as the arbiter of the war should deterrence fail. For many outside the Air Ministry, however, Britain's vulnerability was convincing evidence that there should be no more war. If there should be war, air war must be outlawed.

At the Geneva Disarmament Conference, Britain took the lead in presenting the case for qualitative disarmament, especially air disarmament, if general disarmament could not be agreed. But the discussion of such proposals only increased the fear of air war by showing how easy it would be to get round any such disarmament. How would the international community prevent the conversion of airliners to bombers in a world disarmed of military air forces? How could it prevent the hiding of significant air forces in the outlying areas of Empire, to be recalled at very short notice in the event of new hostilities in Europe? Limiting the size of aircraft or their armaments would not prevent the possibility of the development of 'a bomb as big as a walnut' which could destroy a city. It was in response to the difficulties of air disarmament, and as an attempt to force the pace on the issue, that Stanley Baldwin uttered the most quoted phrase about air war of the interwar years: 'the bomber will always get through.' The only way to win such a war was 'to kill more women and children' with one's own attacks than did one's enemy.[3] Baldwin's speech was planned as an appeal to Europe to rally support for the scheme for air disarmament that Britain was soon to put to the Geneva Disarmament Conference, the so-called MacDonald Plan. The speech was all the more disturbing for the fact that it came from the politician widely considered to be the most honest as well as the most astute of his generation. The Geneva Conference also gave Hitler the opportunity to make his first spectacular foray on the international system, by walking out of the Conference and, a year later, announcing the existence of the Luftwaffe, in defiance of the Versailles restrictions on German armaments. Again, it was Baldwin who gave the fear of air attack quite specific European focus when he declared that, in the age of air power, one no longer thought of the White Cliffs of Dover as the British frontier; one thought of the Rhine.[4]

Britain was not unique in her fear of air war, but the way in which aircraft apparently wholly undermined the country's historic invulnerability to attack turned the bomber into a fixation in this period. A few prescient commentators believed that the fear would prove to be groundless. A.M. Low suggested that the British would get used to bombing, if and when it started, just as so many continental Europeans had got used to the danger of invasion. The threat, he believed, lay in the novelty, a fear of the unknown.[5] An analogy could be drawn with the invasion scares of the years before 1914, when advances made in naval technology were used to whip up public scares that Britain was suddenly open to attack.[6] Certainly a fear of the unknown, part of a new worry about the effects of the application of science and technology, may have been at work here, a natural enough reaction to the slaughter that had occurred in the first of the machine wars, the *Materialschlacht*.

There is an analogy with more recent fears as well: the fear of nuclear attack in the 1950s and 1960s. In both periods the sheer speed of the development of the technology held its own terror, lending an unpredictability to the future, particularly when it was potential enemies who were making the developments. The Americans won the Schneider Trophy for air speed in 1919 with a speed of 107 mph; by 1938, a Luftwaffe Messerschmidt Bf 109 had raised the record to 469 mph. The Americans captured the altitude record in 1920 at 33,000 feet; in 1938, the Italian Air Force reached 56,000 feet. The distance record in 1925 stood at 1967 miles; by 1938 it had been raised to 7158 miles.

Every year, literally, the threat posed by air power grew as aircraft flew higher, faster and further, opening up vast cubic airspaces from which to launch a wholly unexpected attack out of a clear blue sky, as it were. Given the range of options open to attacking bombers, defence appeared virtually impossible. The British air theory pre-echoed the 1950s nuclear doctrine of 'massive retaliation': the only credible preparation against air attack, the RAF argued, was the overpowering counter-offensive. Like the fears of 'missile gaps' in the 1960s, in the 1930s there were fears of discrepancies in front-line air strengths and how they should be calculated, something which Churchill exploited to the full in his rampaging attacks on the scale of air rearmament in Britain.

What was expected to happen if the bombers ever arrived? In thinking the unthinkable, the construction so often used to describe what air war would be like was to imagine the huge artillery bombardments of the Great War visited on civilian targets. Anthony Eden, for instance, described to the House of Commons his own experience of such a bombardment while serving as an infantry officer in France:

> quite suddenly it began to rain bombs for anything from ten minutes to a quarter of an hour. I do not know how many bombs fell in that time, but something between thirty and forty, I suppose. It seemed to us to be hundreds. What rests in my mind is not only my own personal terror, which was quite inexpressible . . . but the comment made when it was over by somebody who said 'There, now you have had your first taste of the next war'.[7]

Civilians, it was assumed, were less able to take it than military personnel, and the result must be a collective shell shock, a national nervous breakdown. The Italian General Giulio Douhet in the 1920s imagined a war between France and Germany in which the French used traditional military methods while the Germans relied on strategic air attack. France, he reckoned, would collapse in a matter of days. The date he chose for this war was 1940, a coincidence that recurs a number of times in contemporary forecasts of what was to come. Douhet's book was in fact first published in English in Britain in 1940, though it had been available through secondary sources since the 1920s.[8]

If civilians were assumed to be weak in a way military personnel were not, class and race bigotry also often inflected the military descriptions of what air war would be like. The pioneer tank expert General J.F.C. Fuller, who was also occasional military spokesman for the British Union of Fascists, reckoned that it would be the Jewish element in the East End of London that would be most likely to panic in an air raid. Group Captain John Slessor, in calculating the likely effect of air attack on France, commented that 'your toothpick worker will probably go to ground'.[9] The British, he seems to have assumed, would not do the same. In fact, the official RAF theory of strategic air war – since it accepted that Britain would not bomb first but only in retaliation – actually depended on the unvoiced understanding that the British would be able to 'take it' longer than the enemy.

The period saw a new public interest in apocalyptic literature, analogous once again to novels such as *On the Beach* from the nuclear era. I.F. Clarke, in analysing such literature, concluded that 1918 marked the fundamental shift in popular writing about war, not 1945 and Hiroshima. The Great War, Clarke argued, marked the point of retreat from the old, aggressive and heroic attitudes to war in popular literature: 'All that has been written about future wars since Hiroshima merely repeats and amplifies what was said between the two world wars. The only difference is the sense of scale.'[10] What the interwar stories reveal is a worry about revolution and about the new weapons of war, but also a connection between these two worries. Books such as *The Red Fury*, *The Red Tomorrow*, and *Against the Red Sky* hardly need to be read to understand the message: the warning is there in the titles. Written from an avowedly reactionary perspective in the first four years of peace, these three novels suggest the strength of quasi-fascist appeals to public opinion in a period when communism was making a measurable impact on European politics. However, the red menace was projected as only one part of the wider threat to civilization as a whole. The kind of fears that had motivated elitist critics of mass culture in the nineteenth century to rail against the materialism of their age – Samuel Taylor Coleridge and Matthew Arnold most obviously – now took on a sharper form in popular literature as the threat of future war. Frankenstein's man-made monster was on the loose and capable of destroying his maker.

Edward Shanks' *People of the Ruins* pictured a Britain returned to tribalism in a ruined industrial landscape, constantly feuding in a series of little wars after the great catastrophe. The symbols are familiar but distanced from a contemporary reader by the myth of 1940; St Paul's, for instance, is not the heroic beacon it became in the Blitz but a heap of ruins.[11] While Shanks' projection of future war in 1920 suggests that the world need do no more than repeat what had happened between 1914 and 1918 to assure its destruction, in the 1930s the stories of future war more typically refer to the destructive potential of new weapons, and aircraft in particular. 'Miles' wrote

The Gas War of 1940 in 1931, while the Geneva Disarmament Conference was in session and at the height of the international financial
crisis that did so much to set the course for the Second World War.
This imaginary war begins with a German invasion of Poland. That
much was probably predictable to the pessimist in 1931, but the date
on which it is imagined to begin is 3 September 1940, a coincidental
conflation of two significant crisis dates in the early years of the war,
the day of the British declaration of war in 1939 and the year of
Britain's attack from the air. Poland is smashed from the air and the
Maginot Line similarly pulverized. London and other great cities of
the world are attacked with high explosives and poison gas; the huge
death-toll is the result not just of the direct effects of the air weapon
but the panic that ensues, with thousands trampled to death in the
congested streets.[12]

In *The Poison War* and *The Black Death* it is again noxious gas that is
projected as the worst part of the horror of the war of the future. The
use of poison gas in the Great War, however inefficient it might have
been according to military historians, appeared in the popular imagination as the most perverted of all the misuses of science in that war, and
its possible use by massed air attack against vulnerable cities in a future
war stood as a kind of paradigm of the death of the pre-1914 assumption of inevitable progress. Science and technology between them had
left the city and the materialist civilization of the nineteenth century
waiting for Apocalypse.

How such wars should be stopped, how humanity is to be redeemed,
is not always clear in such stories. Their function is simply to offer a
warning that some way must be found. More often than not they act
as effective propaganda for the disarmament lobby, and sometimes
for the League of Nations or some similar though more formidable
form of international police force. Their point is that science and technology have become alienated forces, but that they are also man-made
and man must learn how to control them. I use the gender term
advisedly here, as there is an innate criticism of masculinity's projection
of aggression through science and technology. Sometimes the point was
made overtly. G. Cornwallis-West's *The Women who Stopped War*
featured women worldwide, called in to work in factories as a reserve
army of labour in a man-made war, using the strike weapon to enforce
peace.[13] Eric Linklater's *The Impregnable Women* argued that politics
was a male invention to protect selfish interests, whereas female interests lay with the defence of all humanity. So the wives of the politicians
and soldiers collude to bring the war to an end with a sex strike.[14]

That war is a man's game from which women are largely excluded undoubtedly accounts for the popularity of war literature among male readers, who are thereby allowed to participate vicariously in the male solidarity myth, but much of the popular war literature of the years between the wars must have made very uncomfortable reading for men. The exceptions may have been those texts featuring public-school officers in the Great War, which remained fascinated with the cult of self-sacrifice and refused to look forward to its implications for an age of even more destructive weaponry. The very successful stage play *Journey's End* remained ambivalent on this point. Ernest Raymond's *Tell England* was a homoerotic tale of two public school-boys growing up in England before the war, learning the code and then journeying to make the supreme sacrifice at Gallipoli. When it was filmed, however, in the rather different climate of 1931, what emerged was a much more ironic play on the title, specifically the implication that the public-school code had been hideously exploited to continue a pointless war.[15]

For younger public-school writers, caught between one war they had been too young to fight and one for which they would be too old, war retained a hideous fascination. George Orwell believed himself a little less than a man for having missed the Great War, and even explained his decision to go to fight in Spain partly in terms of guilt. About the next war, however, he was unequivocal. The machine men would use their war machines to create the world of 1984. In *Keep the Aspidistra Flying* and *Coming Up for Air,* the bomber plays an important symbolic role as the shape of the future, the 'great death wish of the modern world'.[16] By the time the Second World War was upon him, Orwell could at least hope that the experience would wake up the country which, in the last resort, he simply could not let down:

> the men in bowler hats, the pigeons in Trafalgar Square, the red buses, the blue policemen – all sleeping the deep, deep sleep of England, from which I sometimes fear that we shall never wake till we are jerked out of it by the roar of the bombs.[17]

Cinema tended to be more upbeat on this subject. War made good cinema, and air war better than most, with its opportunities for spectacular aerial photography and stories of derring-do. British cinema could never produce the big budgets necessary to deal effectively with aerial combat, and British audiences seem to have preferred the American product. A number of Hollywood directors were themselves keen pilots and anxious to proselytize 'air-mindedness'. While films such as *All Quiet on the Western Front* dealt solemnly and effectively with the slaughter of the land war, films about aerial combat allowed film-makers to side-step such morbidity. It could still be suggested that the knights in the air had managed to avoid the sordid mud and bullets of the trenches and to retain some of the chivalric glamour of previous wars. *Wings* and *Hell's Angels*, for example, two films that established the popularity of the air combat film, both revolved around love rivalries which threatened to undermine the men and their mission. In *Wings*, two young men fall in love with the same girl. Both join the Air Corps and both become aces in the European war. They remain close, but their respective relationships with the girl threaten their friendship and their mission. One gendered point implied by the story is that women's intrusion into a 'man's world' is a threat to male solidarity. *Hell's Angels* concerns two brothers of very different temperaments. One is a freewheeling womanizer, but he also has a streak of cowardice. The other brother is made of stronger, quieter stuff and attempts to keep his brother in line. Both volunteer for an extremely risky bombing mission for different reasons: the first brother wants to lose his cowardly reputation and the second wants to protect his brother. Which will turn out to be the truer man?[18] Air war is essentially a backdrop to male rivalries in both films. The power to fly confirms masculinity and provides the arena for the protagonists' jousting.

The image of the flying ace clearly has great potential in popular culture; witness the pre-Bondian figure of Bulldog Drummond in popular literature. Both before and since the Second World War, cinema has preferred to concentrate on the war of the individualistic fighter pilots rather than on the morally questionable strategy of bombing, yet in Britain in 1936, Alexander Korda risked the money he had made out of *The Private Life of Henry VIII* to film H.G. Wells' version of the future, *Things to Come*. The film begins with the destruction of London in a devastating air attack. After the initial assaults, a broken-backed war continues in the shambles, led by tin-pot warlords such as the Chief, a thinly veiled caricature of Mussolini in this year of the Italian venture in Abyssinia. Yet, in H.G. Wells' still optimistic view of the world, the bombers that wreaked such destruction may be used to establish a new world order. The airmen establish control over the high technology of air power and use their superiority to enforce peace and rebuild the world. Within a generation, the new order has also developed the ability to travel into space but, as the first astronauts are getting ready to be shot into space by the giant space gun (which resembles a massive Great War howitzer), there is dissent from those citizens who want no more of this dangerous quest for progress.

The film asks us to accept that man must still reach for the stars, however much technology is currently being abused in self-destructive ways.[19] The film was not a commercial success. Perhaps its depiction of the destructive potential of air war was too worrying, especially as the international situation grew increasingly dangerous in the second half of the 1930s. Perhaps its preachy tone in relation to continued techno- logical progress rubbed roughly against sensibilities now increasingly prepared to be dubious about technology.

Apart from fables about the recent war or about the one to follow, cinema also allowed audiences a glimpse of current troubles around the world. Newsreels pictured the Japanese bombing in China, the Italians in Abyssinia and the Condor Legion in Spain. The Gaumont British commentator brought what had happened at Guernica right back home when he warned, with his customary tone of urgency: 'This was a city. These were homes like yours.'[20] Not only did newsreels keep audiences of up to nineteen million a week at least partially informed about foreign events, they also made familiar the leading politicians of the time. The Conservative Party courted the newsreel companies as the easiest access to the mass electorate provided by the franchise of 1918. Baldwin and Chamberlain appeared regularly on newsreels. Chamberlain, in particular, proved an adept performer, the first Chancellor to explain his yearly budget to the cinema audience. From the written archives, Chamberlain emerges as a rational but cold and spiky individual. On newsreel, by contrast, he appears as a sensible, concerned and humane politician, the epitome of common sense. The Conservatives were rewarded for their efforts by the newsreel com- panies with a wholly uncritical projection not only of their leaders, but also of all their policies, including the tricky question of rearma- ment – projected as an unfortunate necessity in an arming world. The greatest triumph for propaganda of all was the extraordinary coverage given by the newsreels to the Munich agreement, Gaumont British offering an almost hysterical endorsement both of the agree- ment and Chamberlain personally. 'One man saved us from the greatest war of all', the commentator proclaims, and 'Posterity will thank God, as we do now, that in our hour of desperate need, our safety was guarded by such a man – Neville Chamberlain.'[21]

Chamberlain had never flown before he went to see Hitler in 1938. He told the Cabinet about the panoramic view of London he had as he flew back with the agreement:

He had imagined a German bomber flying the same course. He had asked himself what degree of protection they could afford for the thousands of homes which he had seen stretched out below him and he had felt that we were in no position to justify waging a war today.[22]

Chamberlain later gave a similar description to the House of Commons. This was by no means his only justification for Munich, but he implied that one had to have a very compelling reason for going to war to risk such an outcome. Czechoslovakia, it was clear, was not such a cause. As Chancellor of the Exchequer as well as Prime Minister, Chamberlain had been sure that the RAF should be at the forefront of British rearmament. Once the Disarmament Conference broke down and rearmament became inevitable in 1934, the Treasury rejected defence advice that the naval threat presented by the Japanese was immediate and pressing, preferring instead to concentrate on the still nascent air threat from Germany. This decision seemed justified in 1935, when the Germans declared that they already had air parity with Britain and were now aiming for air parity with the Soviet Union.

There began a hectic race to increase the front-line strength of the British bomber force as a means of deterring Germany and keeping her talking. This race continued until late 1937 when the Minister for Defence Co-Ordination, Sir Thomas Inskip, reviewing defence expenditure over the next five years, ruled that Britain could no longer afford to keep up. What Britain now needed, he believed, was some sort of defence against air attack, given Germany's lead. It was only at this point that priority was given to Fighter Command over Bomber Command. It was a decision taken in the teeth of strong opposition from the Air Ministry, which believed that decisions such as those taken at Munich were inevitable, given the Germans' capacity to blackmail Europe with the threat of air attack. The Air Staff still did not believe that an effective air defence was possible for Britain. Radar, after all, was still in its infancy and still unproven, and the famous fighters that were to take Fighter Command through the Battle of Britain were only just entering the front line.

The bleak prospect that popular culture drew of a bombing war was matched by official estimates of the casualties that were likely to ensue from German air attack – up to 60,000 a day. This sounds an absurd overestimate in view of German capability at the time. It was based on the calculation that ten tons of bombs would cause ten times more casualties than one ton. Admittedly, reliable evidence was hard to come by when there had as yet been no air raids on the scale

Figure 1 Wigan, 1936. © Hulton Archive.

Figure 2 Chamberlain the Peacemaker, 1938. © Popperfoto.

Two of the most significant photographs in positioning the 1930s in British history. The first, from *Picture Post* (Figure 1), and archived with the enormously influential Hulton Archive, helped to summarize a one-dimensional view of the social problems of the decade. The second signified the supposed futility of appeasement in the post-*Guilty Men* setting (Figure 2). In its original context, however, it was part of the media heroicization of Chamberlain as the common-sense peacemaker.

envisaged, but easily available operational research on the kill rate of small arms and artillery ammunition carried out by the War Office would have shown that this casualty rate was highly unlikely. That such research was not undertaken demonstrates just how different air war was imagined to be. After all, the RAF and USAF were to be able to inflict even greater casualty figures than these on Dresden in early 1945. The figure was nowhere near accurate in the case of the contemporary Luftwaffe, but it was coming within the realms of possibility for air power.

By early 1940, casualty figures had been scaled down to a possible 16,000 deaths a day. What might have been the effect on urban dwellers if such casualty figures had actually occurred? The Home Defence Committee stated bluntly that 'it is obvious that the weight of attack . . . is so great that even if unlimited money and resources were available it would be impossible to prevent heavy casualties and great destruction of property'.[23] For years, the government kept secret that it was even considering civil defence, for fear that the very mention of air raids precautions (ARP) would cause the public panic that it was believed would ensue from air raids. The Air Raids Precautions Bill was not introduced into parliament until November 1937, and was then rushed into law by January 1938. The principle to be applied was that of dispersal: non-essential urban dwellers should be evacuated. Since it was believed that there was likely to be a panic to get out of the cities, this was initially conceived as a police operation. One significant reason for not sending the Army to France in the 1930s was that it might well be needed for civil defence duties at home, particularly since the British Army was at this time one of the most experienced riot control organizations in the world.

As protection against high explosives, families were to be given sectional steel shelters – Anderson shelters as they came to be known – to half-bury in their gardens. The Anderson shelter protected suburbia and that section of the working class fortunate enough to have a garden, but did little for the tenement dweller. This was to be remedied by the provision of the Morrisson shelter after the war had started, though it was not available in any numbers before the Blitz ended. The Labour opposition would have preferred much larger, concrete community shelters, but the ARP Committee ruled them out as too costly in terms of lives if they suffered a direct hit. It has recently been argued that there was a social as well as a psychological dimension to prewar shelter policy, which reflected a deeply demoralized assessment of the common people on the part of the state. Mass shelters, which might have offered greater protection from attack as it was then envisaged, would have required central funding and planning on a much greater scale than the state at that time was prepared to allow, and might also have encouraged the 'deep-shelter mentality', the mass defeatism that government expected would be the response of civilians to attack. Gas attack could be met much more cheaply by the issue of free gas masks to the whole population; thus gas attack was concentrated upon at the expense of shelters.[24]

For incendiary attack, the government could offer only stirrup pumps and advice to keep buckets of sand handy. Thirty-two million pounds over four years was made available from the government to help local authorities to meet the basic provisions of ARP beyond the centrally provided shelters and gas masks. There began, too, the building of a civil defence organization which was finally to include not simply air-raid wardens but an entire alternative state in being, with area civil defence commissioners ready to take over the role of local authorities with dictatorial powers in the event of social or political breakdown.

The provisions that were made now appear paltry, in view of the threat envisaged. In fact they were to serve Britain relatively well in 1940. Evacuation, certainly, was something of a disaster, because it was so poorly organized. So much emphasis had been placed on getting children out of the cities that little thought had been given to the problems of the reception areas, particularly the social mismatches that would result. But evacuation had been designed simply to save lives, and would certainly have saved many thousands of young people if bombing had been as devastating as was envisaged. That evacuation in itself became something of a minor social revolution was one of those unforeseen and unavoidable consequences bequeathed by the 1930s on 1940. Clearly, much more needed to be done, in particular a change in the relationship between central government and local authorities in organizing for those smaller, everyday, practical difficulties of dealing with air raids and post-raid welfare. The emergency services needed to be organized on a national basis.

What prewar civil defence preparations do suggest is that the state had come fatalistically to accept that, if appeasement should fail, there was nothing it could do to prevent massive loss of life, with possibly ruinous attendant problems of law and order. There was little enough evidence on which to work, but there was a real fear. This fear was a product of a depressed faith in industrial democracy as it emerged from the Great War. So many cities, centres of the vibrant, progressive Victorian culture, had been economically depressed since the war, and were now probable targets for large-scale destruction. It was to take a massive psychological effort to transform this wholly depressing prospect into the spirit of a People's War that was to dominate by the end of 1940. The sense of foreboding that coloured predictions is clear. In the trail of the mass destruction that the bomber would wreak, it was widely believed, must come social and even political revolution. To a generation of politicians whose attitudes were framed by the Great War and by the frictions of the Depression, the prospect of class tensions erupting into open warfare was real enough. Too often in the interwar years, widespread rioting had seemed just one more police baton charge away. What would happen if the bombers flew over Jarrow or Merthyr and the flimsy structures of social and political control were broken down?

Preparations for war were framed with these considerations in mind, and on the assumption that the Great War and the Depression had, between them, already created the preconditions for the momentous changes the bombers would bring about. Very few countries in history have deliberately and voluntarily gone into a war in which, it was quite clear, saving the old world order was extremely unlikely.

Some right-of-centre historians have recently come to look more favourably on Chamberlain for foreseeing that Britain could not maintain great-power status after another massive war. They have also come to look less favourably on Churchill for not foreseeing this, and for letting Labour into power in 1945.[25] But, even from a right-wing point of view, it could just as easily be argued that a great deal of Britain's old order was actually saved during the war, and certainly a great deal more than would have been possible if Europe had been dominated by Hitler without some challenge from Britain.

Chamberlain went to war declaring that everything he had fought for in public life was crashing in ruins around him. He at least assured that Britain would go into this war united. Even the pacifist ex-leader of the Labour Party had to admit on the day war was declared that, given Hitler's record, 'we can do no other'.[26] Chamberlain's public virtual admission of personal failure also allowed him to become the scapegoat for the failures of the first nine months of the war. This, of course, did not make the grim facts of the 1930s go away; it merely recontextualized them as a new mythic structure to re-explain the past, the present and the future. 'Peace in our time', the uplifting slogan of the interwar years, had reduced the nation to the point at which she could only be saved by 'blood, toil, tears and sweat', the passwords to national regeneration.

3 To Dunkirk

In *1940: Myth and Reality*, Clive Ponting wrote:

> A study of life in Britain in 1940 shows that the pattern inherited from the 1930s continued almost unchanged and that the government, in seeking to control and organize the country, was deeply conservative, instinctively repressive, suspicious about the willingness of the population to withstand the pressures of war and incompetent in relieving the suffering caused by bombing.[1]

Ponting's book was a deliberate attempt to sensationalize 1940, to tell 'the truth', to uncover 'the lies'. The back cover tells us that 'after fifty years of myth, it is time to face the reality of 1940', a story of ineptitude and propaganda rather than Britain's 'finest hour'. In fact, there was nothing much in the book that was not already known. Certainly, it was already well known that Britain was broke and utterly dependent on the United States. Certainly, many details of the fiasco of the Battle of France did not surface at the time. Certainly, too, Britain did consider a possible peace with Germany in 1940. One is tempted to respond: 'So what?' Counter-factual history does not get us very far. Ponting, anyway, failed to understand what is significant in myths and their making. The myth was made not *primarily* to mislead the British, as Ponting implies, but to help them to survive not just another political mess but the greatest threat in national history. That myth was necessary to help them to make sense of their disaster, and to fight on. The alternative was to come to terms with the Nazis: in the circumstances, whatever was needed, it was not Ponting's notion of 'reality'.

Deliberate lies were rarely spread during the war, anyway: the slogan, rather, was 'the truth, nothing but the truth and, as far as possible, the whole truth'. Governors learned early that it was too dangerous to be caught in a lie: Lord Haw Haw would see to that.

The myth was actually formed on a base of unassailable facts, however much Ponting wants us to look at other facts, which is simply to point us in the direction of another 'potential' myth, another story of 1940 which never became dominant. The dominant myth – or mythic structure, rather, the interconnecting metanarrative of Dunkirk, the Battle of Britain and the Blitz – actually admits many of the mistakes but includes them as counterpoints in a more heroic story. In spite of the ineptitude, Britain survived; the People's War overcame the Guilty Men, and Britain fought on alone when the odds were stacked heavily against her being able to do so.

Yet there is certainly a point to be made about the early reluctance of the government to trust the people. In view of the mythic fear of air warfare, this is not entirely inexplicable. It was very widely believed, not only in Britain but also throughout Europe, that in this kind of war the social control of a panicky population was likely to become a prime concern. The collapse of Belgium, Holland and France in the summer of 1940 prompted the dissemination of rumours of the disruption caused by fifth columnists as an explanation of the rapidity of the collapse. This was a possible foretaste of what might happen in the event of an invasion of Britain. Yet unless a bond of trust was established between nation and state, such worries would become self-validating. The difficulties in the way of establishing just such a trust are clear from the history of the Ministry of Information (M.o.I.), in the early months of the war, and the relationship of state and media through the first crisis of 1940, the retreat from France.

The decision to form such a Ministry in the event of war had been taken in 1935. Sir Stephen Tallents, an intelligent and successful expert in public relations formerly at the Empire Marketing Board, the GPO and the BBC, was appointed its Director-General Designate. The development of the M.o.I. was to prove a major test of the state's ability to mobilize the nation for total war, and to construct a unity of purpose among the people. The Ministry was to have at its disposal, if it learned how to use it, unprecedented possibilities in terms of moulding the public mood. This was the first radio war and, to all intents and purposes, the first cinema war. Newspaper readership was higher than ever before. The development of the advertising industry made available the advertising hoardings, the copywriters, the market research, and all the paraphernalia of the hard-sell that had developed with the consumer economy in the 1930s. Prewar planning was disjointed, however, as few politicians wished to hitch their wagon to an organization whose major role, it was assumed, would be the highly unpopular application of censorship. In fact, the very idea of a Ministry of Information had been severely undermined by revelations through the interwar years of the skulduggery of Beaverbrook's Ministry at the end of the Great War. So successful was the Ministry believed to have been in its lies that it bore responsibility for that public hatred of Germany which was said to have tied politicians' hands in the ensuing peace talks.

Yet, for all the admitted difficulties, what emerges from the prewar preparations is a straightforward amateurishness, the product of public school and Oxbridge civil servants completely out of touch with ordinary people. In spite of, or perhaps because of Tallents' ability, he was not long in the job. Civil servants' tendency in the 1930s to generalize on such topics as the 'British national character' in relation to the next war betray Anglocentric, class-conscious and gendered attitudes. Their typical Briton was a bit of a John Bull: anti-intellectual, rather dull, but fundamentally decent and fair. British women, on the other hand, could be relied upon for their stoicism and their enjoyment of the creature comforts of life. Thus the officers of the Home Publicity Division discussed ways of countering panic during air attacks on the day Germany invaded Poland:

> Lady Grigg said that the most comforting thing – at least where women were concerned – was to have a cup of tea and get together to talk things over.
>
> This was agreed to be a most valuable suggestion. Ways for carrying it into effect . . . were considered. It was decided that some . . . widely spread method was required and that an appeal should be made to householders to supply tea to anyone in their neighbourhood who needed it during or after an air raid.
>
> Professor Hilton . . . referred to the value of sugar for steadying the nerves.[2]

This was most probably true, but it hardly amounted to a psychological insight, particularly in view of the popular conception of the horrors of air attack at the time. Press reaction to the early M.o.I. was typified by the *New Statesman*, which commented that the Ministry was staffed by a 'scramble of socially favoured amateurs and privileged ignoramuses'.[3]

For whatever reasons, the Ministry's first efforts resulted in the most amateurish gaffe. At the outbreak of war, the Ministry decided on an immediate message of reassurance. The result was certainly attention-grabbing: a massive red poster, topped with the crown, which declared '*Your* courage, *your* determination, *your* resolution will bring us victory'. *The Times* commented on such material that 'the insipid and patronizing invocations to which the passer-by is now being treated have a power of exasperation which is all their own'.[4] That first poster campaign of the war also became the subject of a withering attack by Mass Observation (MO), developing the kind of public ridicule which was to bedevil the Ministry for the first two years of its existence and which was to result in the departure of minister after minister. Charles Madge and Tom Harrisson had founded MO in 1937. In what might be called MO's founding manifesto, Madge and Harrisson had spoken of a gap which they felt existed between governors and governed, a fundamental lack of communication and understanding in the relationship between nation and state. MO was designed to analyse the ordinary and the commonplace, to set the 'man-in-the-street' as the subject rather than the object of mass investigation. Unlike Gallup, MO made no claim to a systematic investigation of 'public opinion' by direct questioning. It chose instead to listen to the people through a network of observers and then report what the people were really talking about.

The aim, in short, was to allow public opinion to emerge from the people rather than be guided by questions. In listening to people's reactions to the M.o.I. poster, observers noted that many immediately picked up on the apparent discrepancy between 'you' and 'us', interpreting it cynically to mean that sacrifices would be made by the many for the few. Apart from anything else, a 'resolution', for most, was something you passed at a union meeting and did not seem likely to help the war effort.[5] But Lord Macmillan, first wartime Minister of Information, refused to sanction further research from MO. This may have been a reaction to press grumblings about the expenditure and overstaffing of the Ministry, but it suggested that the Ministry was refusing to accept criticism from the experts, particularly if the experts were considered a little radical in their politics. Lord Reith, former Director General of the BBC, succeeded Macmillan as Minister, somewhat reluctantly, and Churchill in turn dropped him in May 1940. Duff Cooper survived until July 1941 when Churchill's confidant, Brendan Bracken, replaced him. However, from this point the Ministry was to enjoy more stability, largely because it was clear by this time that the professionals in the media could safely be left to get on with their jobs and that the Ministry could and should work with them, not against them.

A major early problem was the public perception of the Ministry as not only ineffectual but also interfering. In December 1939, the former broadcaster Mary Adams was appointed Director of Home Intelligence in the Ministry, her job to provide a continuous flow of information on what the public was thinking. Adam, like Tallents, was an experienced and able public communicator who saw the need for openness to secure public confidence, but the Whitehall culture found such openness difficult. The division was soon asked to take on a whole range of work not just for the M.o.I. but also for the Ministry of Home Security and the Ministry of Food. This widespread demand for information from government departments was in itself healthy, but it overstretched the department. The secrecy of its early work also opened the Ministry to public charges of nosiness when the secret inevitably leaked out. Branded 'Cooper's Snoopers' by the press, the work of the Wartime Social Survey for Home Intelligence seemed to conform to the inquisitorial tendencies against which Britain was supposed to be fighting. The snoopers campaign undoubtedly weakened the Ministry still further in those early days although, in one sense, it actually worked to 'prove' that freedom of the press was not at risk.

The point remained that the work of Home Intelligence simply had to be done if the government was to respond adequately to public needs. In fact, Home Intelligence's own investigation suggested that members of the public were actually in favour of the 'snoopers' and were not at all averse to answering their questions.[6] It was perhaps partly in response to the press campaign that the M.o.I. decided on the more extensive use of non-government agencies such as MO to do their intelligence gathering for them. Known to be politically left-of-centre, the use of MO helped the M.o.I. to shed its image as a haven of hidebound snobs. The methods of investigation used by MO, though often criticized as unreliable, also allowed the M.o.I. to be alerted to a range of public issues which would have gone unnoticed using more orthodox public-opinion-gathering measures. At the same time, the Wartime Social Survey was to be run from the London School of Economics to lend it an air of academic neutrality. The M.o.I. had a number of other sources of home intelligence, the most significant of which was the BBC Listener Research Department, which provided important feedback not just on the reception of government information by listeners but on a wide range of social issues in its efforts to keep the BBC and its listeners in touch with each other. This decentralization of intelligence gathering eventually calmed the press and also assured the M.o.I. of a range of more or less sensitive indicators of the public mood.

The response of the M.o.I. to criticism of its intelligence gathering refutes the suggestion that the state was simply complacent in its response to the crisis of war. The demand for information on public opinion from government departments grew rapidly, suggesting an early understanding of the political significance of mass involvement in the new kind of war. Where the M.o.I. was wrong was in assuming that the intelligence gathering should be secret. The traditional civil service attitude that government was a matter for Whitehall and should not be open to public discussion was blown open by the press in its self-appointed role as leader of 'public opinion'. Once the secret was out, non-state agencies – even mildly 'alternative' ones such as MO – were to be included in a wide-ranging exercise of listening to the people.

Though it began as a conservative institution, the Ministry was to evolve into one of the most progressive of government departments, one of the earliest disseminators of the view that the war should be portrayed as a crusade, and that this crusade should include publication of peace aims, which should in turn include measures of social reconstruction. As the demands of war forced the Ministry to draft in personnel who were not career civil servants, a more liberal and liberating attitude emerged towards censorship and, more generally, towards trusting the people to deal with the truth. Churchill was to become increasingly worried that political radicals had infiltrated the Ministry, and part of the reason for sending Bracken to the Ministry was to keep a close eye on such developments.

Above all, the early problems of the M.o.I. were a function of the fact that Chamberlain's wartime government was itself ineffectual and given to offering disastrous hostages to fortune. Bricks cannot be made without straw. While the phony war left few opportunities or even the need for public exhortation, the public was apparently staggered by the extent of the disaster in Norway, especially after Chamberlain's claim that Hitler had 'missed the bus'.[7] The M.o.I. clearly had not been kept informed by the service ministries of what was happening, and had been given no opportunity to prepare the public. During the rest of 1940, the M.o.I. was involved in a continuous tussle with the service ministries to release information on a much more liberal basis. This entailed very severe practical problems for both the military and the propagandists. The speed of the German advance through the Low Countries and France was unprecedented, so much so that sound information was unreliable after just a few hours. In the equally unprecedented air war that followed, the Air Ministry was understandably reluctant to give out information when it had no real means of telling whether it might be useful to the enemy (for example, the fact that they might have bombed the wrong target). In May 1940 confusion was compounded by the simultaneous political changes in Britain. From this point, a more decisive pattern emerged in both official and unofficial projections of the war.

On Saturday 11 May, the news media had two huge stories on which to lead from the events of the previous day: the invasion of Holland and Belgium and the replacement of Chamberlain by Churchill as Prime Minister. It was to be crucial to the development of the myth that the two events occurred simultaneously: the first made public criticism of the latter virtually impossible. In turn, Churchill's status as the loudest opponent of appeasement in the 1930s could provide a focus for understanding what was happening in Western Europe. There were many serious doubts in high places about Churchill as Prime Minister, but such doubts found no public expression. While Home Intelligence found that many people were perplexed that Churchill's appointment did not immediately change the military situation, within weeks of the beginning of the Battle of France the public seemed to have settled into an understanding that they could not expect miracles. On 11 May, the *Manchester Guardian*, hardly a tradi-tional supporter of Churchill, described the new Prime Minister as a man with 'the boldness, the imagination, the sense of social justice, the capacity to rouse the enthusiasm and devoted service' that would bring the nation through, and the only Conservative with whom Liberals and Labour would willingly work. On Holland and Belgium, the leader writer declared that no countries had ever worked harder to retain their neutrality, and that the invasion would finally show other countries 'what sort of Europe, what sort of world, what despotism of fraud and hate and force' Hitler's victory would impose.[8] Finally, it seemed, the news media had something to get their teeth into.

In the *Daily Express*, David Low pictured Churchill with his new Cabinet rolling up their sleeves and marching forward grimly together, to the legend, 'All behind you Winston.' Within two weeks, however, the news was much more frightening. On 24 May the *Express* reported that the British Expeditionary Force (BEF) was fighting with 'backs to the sea' for the Channel ports. There was no attempt to minimize the dangers:

> German mechanized troops are firing across the cobbled streets of Boulogne. Calais is half an hour's drive – if the Germans can reach it. And the distance from Calais to Dover is twenty-two miles. For four days now these marauding columns have been raiding towns near the coast without serious opposition. At certain points they have penetrated to the rear of the Allied armies in Belgium in an attempt to disrupt their communications.

A map made the dangers all too clear: the advanced German troops were actually closer to British shores than the BEF itself. To a country which knew the Somme area only too well from the blood-letting of twenty-four years before, and which had begun to know the French ports from day trips in the 1930s, the news was indeed appalling. At the bottom of the page, Duff Cooper was quoted as saying that Britain was in one of the most dangerous situations she had ever faced: '"It is no good belittling it or trying to minimize it", he said, "we are facing fearful risks. The British people, when they are up against it, are always prepared to face risks. They would rather know than be kept in the dark".' Cooper even seemed to concede the possibility of imminent defeat in France, adding that 'we still have the integrity of this island, our vast superiority at sea and our Fleet to defend us'. The rest of the *Express* front page was given over to the arrest of Sir Oswald Mosley while, in the centre of the page, members of the British Union of Fascists were photographed giving fascist salutes as they were led away under arrest.[9] The *Express* was to be the most prominent of the newspapers identifying the danger of the fifth column, though even their campaign was to quieten down later in the year as surveys showed that many followed the *Daily Mirror* in resenting the assumption that British society was simply a nest of potential traitors. The extent of the external danger meant that any hint of an internal danger should be narrowly focused. Unfortunately, this may have rebounded on many entirely blameless aliens, some of whom had already fled Hitler's Europe, only to be interned in Churchill's Britain.

The *Express'* front page on 24 May was hardly reassuring stuff. Throughout the Battle, newspaper reporting did nothing to attempt to convince the public that victory was certain; indeed, far from it. *The Times* allowed itself occasional headlines like 'BEF sweeps on' but covered itself with the caution that there was not much hard news to comment upon.[10] Often, the press printed British, French and German communiqués, as if leaving readers to make up their own minds. All the news reporters in France were censored by the military, but most were so far from any real fighting that they had nothing to report anyway. If reporting was confused and confusing, so was the Battle. The Allied command system proved too slow and cumbersome to cope with the fluid methods of attack adopted by the Germans. The French decision to sack General Gamelin and replace him with General Weygand, on 20 May, produced a crucial vacuum of command that prevented what might have been a devastating counter-attack, which might have left the spearhead of the German attack utterly stranded. The German tanks were able to move at great speed – often between forty and sixty miles a day during this attack – but the *Wehrmacht* lacked motorized infantry to back them up.

What is now established as one of the classic military campaigns of modern history could quite easily have become a farcical story of miscalculation by the panzer commanders. As it was, they reached the outskirts of Calais and Boulogne on 22 May, after just twelve days, and on 24 May stopped just fifteen miles short of Dunkirk to allow the infantry to consolidate behind them. Just how the BEF could have escaped, if it had not been for that halt, is difficult to determine. The BEF had begun to retreat on 16 May, as the German advance began to threaten their line of communication. So little involved were the British in the initial but virtually decisive part of the campaign that they suffered only 500 casualties in the first eleven days: in fact, many soldiers of the BEF were never to fire a shot in combat. On 16 May, Churchill asked for preparations to begin for a possible evacuation: plans were ready within three days, and 28,000 troops were to be brought back from France before the main evacuation from Dunkirk began on 27 May. The evacuation was protected by Belgian and then by French troops who were oblivious of the British withdrawal until 29 May. By 4 June the British rearguard had been withdrawn, but the French held on to the perimeter at Dunkirk for two days after the last British soldiers had been evacuated. The War Office had hoped to bring out between 50,000 and 100,000 men, but in fact 225,000 British soldiers had been evacuated. Half as many French came back with them, on their way back to France to resume the battle beyond the German-occupied zone. Britain's only two remaining fully formed divisions also went over to reinforce the 15th Highland Division, left behind by the major evacuation. They surrendered on 12 June, though 136,000 soldiers were to evade capture through further evacuation.[11]

The evacuation from Dunkirk was carried out largely in secret, a secret kept even from French allies for two days, and from the British public for four days, by which time over half the British force had returned to Britain. Even some junior members of the government did not know: Harold Nicolson, Parliamentary Under-Secretary at the M.o.I., noted in his diary on 29 May that Britain 'hoped to evacuate a few of our troops' when the operation was already two days old. When it did become clear what was happening, the media moved into rapid action to provide editorial comment, aided by a military

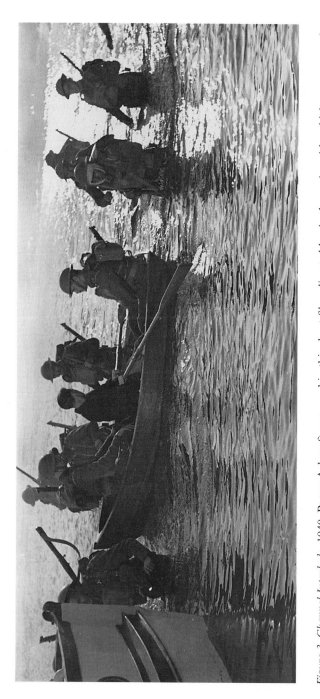

Figure 3 *Channel Interlude*, 1940. Peggy Ashcroft appeared in this short film, directed by Anthony Asquith, which was among the very first to heroicize the 'little boats' of Dunkirk. © Imperial War Museum.

anxious to evade criticism. The first news of the evacuation came on 31 May. 'Tens of thousands safely home already', declared the *Daily Express*: 'through an inferno of bombs and shells the BEF is crossing the Channel from Dunkirk – in history's strangest armada', the first hint of the miracle of the little boats, 'all sizes, all shapes'.[12] The BBC put a brave face on it: 'from the many reports of their arrival and of interviews with the men, it is clear that if they have not come back in triumph, they have come back in glory.' Since the British had not done much of the fighting, it was easily assumed that defeat must have been the result of the weaknesses of Britain's allies. The Director of Military Intelligence with the BEF, General Mason-Macfarlane, reportedly blamed the defeat to journalists on the fact that the French had been outfought and the British consequently left high and dry though undefeated.[13]

Such observations dominated newspaper analyses on 29 and 30 May, though some did point out that it was the braveness of the French defence of the Dunkirk perimeter that allowed so many British to get away. But it was in a spirit of relief rather than scapegoatism that the *Daily Mirror* published its celebrated editorial on Dunkirk: 'Bloody Marvellous.' There was no triumphalism here either, just a sense that, bad as it was, it could easily have been a great deal worse. It was this same spirit of relief that infused Bernard Stubbs' moving BBC commentary from Dover as he watched the evacuated men entrain:

> It was astounding to walk along carriage after carriage full of soldiers and to find in each one – silence. . . . In the dining cars they sat, most of them with their heads on the tables or on pillows improvised out of their equipment. Train after train puffed out of the station, all full of sleeping men. All the way along the line, the people of England stood at the level crossings and in the back gardens to wave to them. And so the men of the BEF came home.[14]

Whoever was to blame, and even if they had left all their heavy equipment behind them, the boys had come home.

The notion that the French were to blame grew in the ensuing weeks. The speed with which the Germans dealt with the rest of France, the ease with which the French accepted the armistice, served to confirm the view that the BEF had been badly let down. The French could tell a different story: of perfidious Albion, of Gort's apparent preference for retreat rather than counter-attack, of the secrecy of the evacuation from Dunkirk, of the refusal to commit more air support. Pétain pointedly reminded Churchill on 11 June that he had committed forty divisions to save the British army at the time of the German spring offensive in 1918, and asked where were the British divisions to save the French now.[15] In the aftermath of the defeat, the British were to add insult to injury by sinking the French fleet to prevent it from falling into German hands. But a defeated France, occupied for four years, could not tell that alternate story. Many French commentators at the time explained the roots of defeat in terms of the domestic politics of the 1930s rather than by looking at the details of what had happened in 1940.[16]

France's defeat, and Britain's subsequent survival, not only worked to confirm Britain's sense of innate national superiority but also helped to cement a more general distrust of European entanglements for generations. It could easily have been otherwise. Just before the débâcle, the Foreign Office had virtually committed itself to a firm Anglo–French alliance after the war, an admission that after the experience of the interwar years Britain could no longer simply stand outside Europe. As defeat stared them in the face, Britain actually suggested an Act of Union with France to try to prevent a moral collapse in Paris. Of course, this was an act of desperation, but it underlines the changes that would have been forced in Britain's attitude to Europe if France had not collapsed. All that this might have implied for the international future of Britain disappeared in seven weeks in the summer of 1940. Willy-nilly, Britain was alone, and was soon to be utterly dependent on a benevolent United States for survival. The French, temporarily 'our brave ally', became defeatists from whose weakness the BEF had been extricated by 'the miracle of Dunkirk'.

There were other culprits to be found nearer home. In the early months of 1940 there developed a profound change in ways of imaging the 1930s. This change developed first among the élite of the intelligentsia, but it spread widely through the mass media to become virtually an unquestioned assumption before the end of the year. There had always been a literature of protest during the 1930s, of course. Walter Greenwood's *Love on the Dole* had appeared in 1931 and was soon being hailed as a model of proletarian literature. The writings and politics of the Auden-Spender group had made them well known as a radical élite, and Auden's description of the 1930s as 'the low dishonest decade' was soon to become one of the favourite popular historical clichés. The Left Book Club had enjoyed a significant though still small circulation during the decade, criticizing a range of contemporary social and international policies, but it was not until 1940 that such attitudes became mainstream. They also became more muted, politically Left-liberal in inclination but certainly

not radical. Malcolm Muggeridge's *The Thirties*, and Robert Graves
and Alan Hodge's *The Long Weekend*, both published early in 1940,
pictured the interwar period as a prolonged abstention from reality,
and the political Left as just as vapid as the dominant Right.[17]

The Battle of France gave such commentaries a distinct and direct
political edge, of a far more practical kind than that of the high-falutin
Marxist critiques of the previous decade. Quite simply, failed politics
had brought Britain to the edge of catastrophic defeat, perhaps even
invasion and distinction as a nation. In *Guilty Men*, 'Cato' (three
journalists of the Beaverbrook press, Michael Foot, Frank Owen and
Peter Howard) made it quite clear where the blame should lie.
Published just a month after Dunkirk, the book opened on the
French beaches with the evacuating troops:

> They were heroes; but heroism is not enough in this world of air
> power and seventy-ton tanks. . . . That night a miracle was born.
> This land of Britain is rich in heroes. She had brave, daring men
> in her Navy and Air Force as well as in her Army. She had
> heroes in jerseys and sweaters and old rubber boots in all the fish-
> ing ports of Britain. That night the word went round.
>
> In a few hours the channel was thick with barges, tugs, small
> coastal vessels, motor boats, lifeboats, private yachts, several
> hundred ships of all sizes and shapes sailing alongside British
> destroyers and sometimes beneath the protection of British
> fighters. It was still a small, the slenderest of hopes.[18]

It had been a matter of flesh against steel, 'the story of an Army
doomed *before* it took the field'. From the beaches, the authors took
the reader back to 1929 as the real beginning of the story, an alliance
between Ramsay MacDonald and Stanley Baldwin to keep Lloyd
George out of power, his offence being that he wanted to do *something*.
First in turn and then together, MacDonald and Baldwin had ruled
Britain for an age, and brought the country to the edge of national
annihilation. Eden and Duff Cooper had been dismissed when they
could no longer tolerate the complacent betrayal of British interests,
and all this time Churchill was kept out because he had no judgement
and wanted office.

There followed a record of the failure of the 1930s, of the fate of the
unemployed certainly, but largely centred on the sell-outs of appeasement. Finally, MacDonald and Baldwin give way to Chamberlain in
1937. The country breathed a sigh of relief, believing that 'something
much better must come since there could be nothing worse'.[19] But

Chamberlain took Britain to Munich and an exhibition of mass hys-
teria in the House of Commons as 'honourable and right honourable
gentlemen yelled and screamed like football fans',[20] itself a telling
classist comment from such a trio of liberals. Chamberlain actually
trusted Hitler, and for six months after Munich believed that the
tiger had been tamed, and the great mass of the politicians also, pathe-
tically, believed him: 'Mr J.H. Thomas, after careful cogitation and
after dinner too, stood up and gave forth: "I believe there will be no
war".'[21] With the invasion of the rump of Czechoslovakia in the
spring of 1939, appeasement was dead, but it still took fifteen months
to lie down.

   Chamberlain was not the only villain of the piece. The entire government was infected with the complacency and self-satisfaction that
Chamberlain exuded, from Sir Thomas Inskip as Minister for the
Co-Ordination of Defence (a job which certainly should have gone to
Churchill rather than to that 'bum-faced evangelical'[22]) to Leslie Burgin
as Minister of Supply, to Ernest Brown as Minister of Labour,
and including all those civil servants who strangled with red tape,
those who desired to take determined and drastic action. Meanwhile,
Parliament remained acquiescent under the dead hand of Captain
Margesson, the Government Chief Whip. Then, on 3 April 1940, after
all the evidence of the power of Germany in the destruction of Poland,
Chamberlain proclaimed that he was ten times more confident than he
had been at the beginning of the war that Britain would win: Hitler had
missed the bus. The result was to be the entire British Army left dirty,
tired and helpless on a French beach. The French in turn were left to
battle hopelessly on against German tanks of a French design made
in the Skoda works of Czechoslovakia. Now Churchill had replaced
the complacent Chamberlain as Prime Minister and had behind him
the united determination of the country.

> But one final and absolute guarantee is still imperatively demanded
> by a people determined to resist and conquer: namely, that the men
> who are now repairing the breaches in our walls should not carry
> along with them those who let the walls fall into ruin. . . . Let
> the guilty men retire, then, of their own volition, and so make an
> essential contribution to the victory upon which all are implacably
> resolved.[23]

Guilty Men was a book in the style of an old-fashioned political
pamphlet, worthy of one of Michael Foot's heroes, Jonathan Swift.

Its methods were satire, parody and humiliation. There was no Franco-phobia here, and only one early reference to the 'perfidy' of the King of the Belgians. This was essentially a domestic drama that had been brewing for eleven years. It was published by Gollancz in the same kind of format as the Left Book Club editions of the 1930s as 'Victory Books No 1', but its politics were far removed from those of earlier Left Book Club editions. On the one hand, behind the scenes, the bumbling politicians had been supported by the banks, big business, the Church, the duchesses, proto-fascists and so on. On the other hand, there was none of the previous anti-imperialism of Gollancz's publications. Indeed, one major complaint made by *Guilty Men* was that the huge resources of the Empire were not rallied by Chamberlain and his cronies, and the book's support for Winston Churchill was hardly typical of the Marxist line. What had happened was that the major figures in the Left Book Club, Harold Laski, John Strachey, and Gollancz himself, had fallen out with the Communist Party over the Nazi–Soviet pact and the communist policy of 'revolutionary defeatism' that followed. Strachey, after a visit to the United States, had become convinced that the New Deal offered a model of an evolutionary road to socialism to replace the failed European Marxist models. In short, the Left Book Club was coming in from the cold, joining the mainstream non-communist British Left in the belief that the system could be reformed from within.

The decline of Marxism, after the brief but well publicized fashionable interest in the 1930s, allowed many other extremely able propagandists for the Left to enter the mainstream of British political and social commentary. Orwell had already announced his conversion to patriotism but, as he pointed out, that did not mean support for Chamberlain's version of England.[24] Britain's entry into the war put her directly in the front line against fascism. This made her worth fighting for, whatever her inadequacies, particularly from the early summer of 1940 when Britain was left to face Hitler alone. For the leftist writers, that made Churchill – of all people – more acceptable than Chamberlain. The departure of Chamberlain and the inclusion of Labour in the new government suggested that the social revolution might be about to begin. Dunkirk provided the fulcrum to lever a potential major shift in national political outlook because it 'proved', dramatically and powerfully, that the old ways simply could not be continued.

So where was regeneration to come from? From the new government, obviously – once it was cleared of the remaining Guilty Men –

but mainly from the people, those 'people of England' whom Bernard Stubbs had watched on the railway crossings and in the back gardens cheering the sleeping men on their way back from Dunkirk. Most dramatically, the notion of national regeneration through the people was highlighted in June 1940 in the stories of the little boats that had supposedly rescued the BEF. The first request for small boats to be made available to the Royal Navy Volunteer Reserve (RNVR) had been issued by the BBC earlier in the Battle of France as government information at the end of the news broadcast. The BBC had not made clear the purpose of the request at the time. Civilians had consequently volunteered their boats but not themselves, and most of the small boats used at Dunkirk were manned by the Royal Navy or RNVR.

Not until the BBC announcement of the evacuation on 31 May did civilian volunteers emerge in numbers. Many of the small boats, not constructed for deep water, could not even be towed successfully across the Channel. Those that did make it across found that they could not easily operate on the shallow beaches at Dunkirk. It is well known that the large majority of the troops that were brought home were taken off the harbour by the Royal Navy. That does not dispose of the 'little boats' as irrelevant. In fact, they did sterling work ferrying men to the larger ships that could not get close enough to the beach. But even that is not the point. The point of the stories is to show that the British national family, with its sons in desperate circumstances, was not prepared simply to leave it to the professionals. When Cato wrote of 'heroes in jerseys and sweaters and old rubber boots' he was playing with a potent national self-image of Britain as a maritime nation, as a people who loved to 'go down to the sea in ships. . . . These men see the works of the Lord: and his wonders in the deep.' There is something deemed particularly honest and simple about the fisherman in British culture. So used to battling with nature, the image of the fisherman using his skills to rescue men under threat from shells and bombs was a particularly telling one.

The little boats were not all fishing boats, of course; in fact, the potency of the stories lies in their diversity: tugs, barges, cruisers, pleasure steamers and so on. J.B. Priestley's first Postscript, broadcast on the BBC on 5 June 1940 just as the evacuation ended, concentrated on the 'Englishness' of the débâcle, the 'way in which, when apparently all was lost, so much was gloriously retrieved'. Priestley concentrated on the pleasure steamers, so redolent of summer holidays before the war, that 'long weekend' whose values the British had to give up if they were to win.

They liked to call themselves 'Queens' and 'Belles'; and even if they were new, there was always something old-fashioned, a Dickens touch, a mid-Victorian air about them . . . these 'Brighton Belles' and 'Brighton Queens' left that innocent foolish world of theirs – to sail into the inferno, to defy bombs, shells, magnetic mines, torpedoes, machine-gun fire – to rescue our soldiers. Some of them – alas – will never return. Among those paddle steamers that will never return was one that I knew well, for it was the pride of our ferry service to the Isle of Wight – none other than the good ship 'Gracie Fields' . . . She has paddled and churned away – for ever. But now – look – this little steamer, like all her brave and battered sisters, is immortal. She'll go sailing proudly down the years in the epic of Dunkirk. And our great grand-children, when they learn how we began this War by snatching glory out of defeat, and then swept on to victory, may also learn how the little holiday steamers made an excursion to hell and came back glorious.[25]

It is mawkish, but it is good. Priestley had mastered a populist and chatty style, and retained at least a shadow of a regional accent, that made his broadcasts virtually revolutionary in the usually starchy context of BBC output. How fitting that the paddle steamer should have been named after that working-class heroine of the 1930s, the 'Lancashire Britannia', though it was somewhat unfortunate that the real Gracie had left Britain quietly but hurriedly for the US with her husband a few days previously, somewhat tarnishing her reputation. It does not matter that the 'Gracie Fields' was in reality *HMS Gracie Fields* on 29 May, technically a minesweeper with her former crew now wearing uniform. When she was bombed, her engine room exploded. She began churning in huge circles, one paddle gone and her rudder jammed. The soldiers she was carrying were taken off, but the *Gracie Fields* sank as she was being towed home. Passenger ferries that had previously worked between Britain and Europe and Ireland were also there, still civilian, with incongruous and largely useless Lewis guns somewhere on their superstructure.[26]

On the morning of Priestley's talk, newspapers and the BBC had given full coverage to one of Churchill's great perorations of 1940, delivered in the House of Commons the previous night. He had warned that wars are not won by evacuations, that Dunkirk was a colossal military disaster, that invasion might be imminent. He continued: 'We shall fight on the beaches, we shall fight on the landing grounds, we shall fight in the fields and in the streets, we shall fight in the hills; we shall never surrender.' Between Churchill and Priestley that day, the war began to make sense as an eventual victory made all the more glorious for the fact that Britain had been brought so low. There is, after all, a way of making disaster sound glorious without even denying that it is disaster. Now Britain had a chance to redeem herself. Churchill's patrician, rotund rhetoric may have stirred the nation in the morning, but, in the evening, Priestley's populist, emotive self-congratulation assured that the *Gracie Fields* had sacrificed herself to allow Britain to fight on. That was what had been salvaged from Dunkirk by the little boats, their incongruity in that savage military setting constituting a 'super-reality' about Britain in crisis.

While new broadcasters like Priestley quickly learned to adopt a populist style, the M.o.I. and politicians – with the obvious exception of Churchill – still had major difficulties with 'you' and 'us'. The M.o.I.'s first poster campaign after Churchill became Prime Minister featured a portrait photograph of Churchill with his words 'Let Us Go Forward Together', but the 'Us' that stood behind him were still symbols of the armed forces – tanks and aircraft – rather than the people. Anthony Eden, talking on radio on 26 June about the possibility of invasion, was positively contorted in his use of 'I', 'you' and 'we'. What emerges as a result is pure hot air rather than a construction of national community:

> We are confident that the enemy will be beaten off, and I will tell you why. Your character is the first reason for my complete confidence. We know that you will never flinch. . . . The world has nowhere to look but to us for the salvation of the precious heritage of civilization which must inevitably pass from Europe unless we, and our brothers from overseas, show the invincible will to defend it. Those over whom the iron wheels of the conqueror have passed, those whom the conqueror now begins to threaten, alike base their hopes on our victory. We shall not fail them.[27]

The problem was that obscure concepts such as those used by Eden – even 'freedom' – meant little in practical terms to most people. What they needed was something more concrete. The government could not afford to leave the civilian population without powerful leadership and constant attention, but by simply increasing the number of talks by ministers on radio, or by putting out threepenny pamphlets, little was achieved. If anything was to be done, all the new resources that had developed since the last war had to be brought into play.

Radio, however, was clearly a very good starting point. This was the first real radio war; indeed, for the larger part of the population, the war actually began on the radio with Chamberlain's broadcast to the nation at 11.15 a.m. on 3 September 1939. By 1940, well over 90 per cent of the population had access to radio, and the BBC had easily overtaken the press as the prime purveyor of news. The significance of the mediating role played by radio in this war cannot be over-estimated. The speed with which news could be broadcast made this war a much more immediate event than any previous one. This put the BBC in an enormously powerful position to influence public constructions of the war and, as a result, its news output was closely monitored by the M.o.I.; in fact, virtually all BBC wartime output was either scripted or pre-recorded. As the BBC began to take the advice of its Listener Research Department, the hierarchy started to introduce a rather less formal style. Already during 1939, after Reith's departure from the BBC, radio had begun to shed some of its formality and reserve.

The demands of war in turn pushed the Corporation to adopt a more personalized approach, to accept that the audience was not just the public but a market, to accept that it could not hope to lead and to form public opinion unless it also gave the impression that it reflected public taste. Priestley was one early example of this, though one that was soon to be controversial. Another example was the practice begun in July 1940 of newsreaders introducing themselves by name, partly so that listeners could distinguish the real thing from the German 'black' broadcasts. The result was that newsreaders like Alvar Liddell and Frank Phillips became household names, itself an important element in the securing of public trust.

The BBC and the M.o.I. had been alarmed in the early months of the war by the apparent popularity of Lord Haw Haw. Home Intelligence, BBC Listener Research and MO had all discovered that many people found Radio Hamburg at least as interesting as the BBC, with up to 30 per cent of the population regularly tuning in to the alternative news that followed the BBC's prime listening slot, the 9 o'clock news on Sunday evenings. The M.o.I. decided that the best way to deal with this was to relax news censorship; better that the British people should hear of disasters from the BBC rather than from the enemy.[28] At the same time, the BBC looked for a popular broadcaster who could keep the interest of the audience. The result was the *Postscripts* programme, dominated through the second half of 1940 by J.B. Priestley who, in twenty weekly broadcasts, established himself as Britain's first radio personality. Priestley's talks continued through the summer and into the Blitz. It was estimated that over 30 per cent of the population tuned in to hear him, though it was never clear that this was the same 30 per cent who had previously tuned in to Lord Haw Haw.

Over the broadcasts a pattern began to emerge, of a mildly alternative history and a mildly alternative future for Britain. It was a Britain of community spirit, which Priestley described as nothing new, but rooted deep in the past. Of his first night on duty as a Local Defence Volunteer on the Downs, he said:

> I felt . . . up there a powerful and rewarding sense of community; and with it too a feeling of deep continuity. There we were, ploughman and parson, shepherd and clerk, turning out at night, as our forefathers had before us to keep watch and ward over the sleeping English hills and fields and homesteads.[29]

From this Hardyesque view of 'Deep England', Priestley turned to the political consequences of mass involvement, a return to the sense of community:

> Now, the war, because it demands a huge collective effort, is compelling us to change not only our ordinary, social and economic habits, but also our habits of thought. We're actually changing over from the property view to the sense of community, which simply means that we realize that we're all in the same boat.[30]

There were rumblings from conservative circles, especially when it became clear that the reconstruction theme was to continue to figure prominently. By October, Priestley was off the air, and, although he returned briefly in 1941, the popular rumour was that the reactionaries had pushed him out. Nevertheless, Priestley had entered British folk culture. His popularity reflected the fact that, with the exception of Churchill, neither the M.o.I. nor the BBC had found anyone to manage the public mood, to make sense of the crisis. Like Churchill, Priestley was the outsider who had pushed himself inside. One commentator has suggested that 'those who enjoyed Priestley's broadcasts were just as likely to enjoy Churchill's. They did not speak to different audiences but to different impulses in the same listeners.'[31] Churchill, in his broadcast of 14 July, also hinted at a People's War:

> This is no war of chieftains, of dynasties or national ambition; it is a War of peoples and of causes. There are vast numbers not only in

Figure 4 Dawn Guard, 1940. 'Coo, look at that Dunkirk. Weren't no un-employed there. Each man had a job to do and he done it.' Two Home Guards, Percy Walsh and Bernard Miles, reminisce and speculate about the future. © Imperial War Museum.

this island but in every land, who will render faithful service in this War, but whose names will never be known, whose deeds will never be recorded. This is a War of the Unknown Warriors.[32]

But Churchill did not draw the implications that Priestley drew. True, Priestley was no radical, but he appeared so in such a setting. His talks were reassuring rather than challenging, an appeal for what he regarded as the fundamental decency of ordinary British people to overcome the machine men. What worried the establishment was that he saw machine men at home, not just on the other side of the North Sea. Who did he mean? In 1940, his targets were likely to have been read as not just the Guilty Men but the faceless bureaucrats who still did not quite trust the 'innate' British sense of decency and fair play, and who might still thwart the liberalization signalled by the war, by the near defeat, and by the new government.

In a similar vein to Priestley was the M.o.I. film *Dawn Guard*, made by the Boulting brothers in the summer of 1940. In terms of the output of the Films Division of the M.o.I., *Dawn Guard* was a transitional film, standing half-way between their laughably unrealistic early material, featuring heroic middle-class spinsters and villainous German spies, and the poetic documentaries that began to dominate by the end of the year with the formation of the Crown Film Unit. *Dawn Guard* featured two Local Defence volunteers, played by Bernard Miles and Percy Walsh, standing on a hilltop guarding the English countryside and bemoaning the threat to this peaceful way of life posed by the war. The younger man reminds the older that the threat is there because 'we all got too lazy':

> 'Coo, look at that Dunkirk. Weren't no unemployed there. Each man had a job to do and he done it. And that's what we got to see they have in peacetime – a job. . . . There mustn't be no more chaps hanging around for work that don't come. No more slums neither. No more dirty, filthy back-streets and no more half-starved children with no room to play in. . . . We can't go back to the old ways of living, leastways not all of it. That's gone forever, and the sooner we make up our minds about that the better.'[33]

In the Boultings' as in Priestley's Local Defence volunteers, John Bull had been translated into a left-liberal yokel, kind at heart, but determined that the mistakes which had brought the country to its present impasse should not be repeated.

Priestley's *Postscripts* and the Boultings' *Dawn Guard* were not radical texts. The values of 'Deep England' to which they appealed would have been perfectly acceptable to any traditional pastoralist, probably including Stanley Baldwin, who regularly used such images and rhetoric to justify the status quo in the interwar years.[34] What was new about them was their context, what they meant in the void created in May 1940 by the collapse of the interwar political coalition and the massive nature of the military defeat in France. What was involved was a form of bricolage, an appropriation, which was also what made these representations so difficult to counter. At the same time, the popularity of *Guilty Men* as an explanation of the military catastrophe can be read as a willingness to understand that there was nothing wrong with Britain as a nation, only with the men who had run it for the previous decade.

Central to the mythic structure of 1940 is the view of the interwar years associated with it, the sense of 1940 as a new beginning. What gave this formulation of the crisis its particular strength was that it offered an explanation and a pattern, something to hang on to through the most disturbing and confusing events, particularly when it was clear that there was worse to come. In June 1940, the many were represented as reasserting their primacy over the elite, as politicians from Left and Right forcing the Guilty Men out of power, but also as civilian sailors in little boats, as 'the people of England' welcoming the soldiers back, as home guards watching the sun come up over the historic fields and hedgerows. They emerged as symbols of democratic regeneration, of an opportunity, which also involved a warning:

> If apathy and stupidity return to reign once more; if the privileges of the few are seen to be regarded as more important than the happiness of many; if a sterile obstruction is preferred to creation; if our faces are still turned towards the past instead of towards the future; if too many of us simply will not trouble to know, or if we do know, will not care, then the great opportunity will pass us by, and soon the light will be going out again.[35]

4   Invasion and the Battle of Britain

'Now we know where we are', yelled a tugboat skipper across the Thames, 'no more bloody allies!'[1] 'Very well, alone!' shouted David Low's cartoon soldier from the White Cliffs of Dover, shaking his fist across the Channel.[2] But the fall of France upset all the calculations on which Britain had based her strategy for fighting a war with Germany. If the bombing which Britain was to endure later in the war was actually a great deal less disastrous than had been forecast before the war, the situation in the summer of 1940 was infinitely worse than anything that had been expected.

Already the German move into Scandinavia had opened a naval problem in the North Sea and a possible base for long-range air operations against the North East and Scotland. The loss of the whole of the Channel coast and the Bay of Biscay was a naval catastrophe. Even if Germany did not use the opportunity to invade Britain, maintaining supplies to a nation which relied utterly on imports would be extremely difficult as a result of the Battle of France. The major port of London could only be reached by hazardous routes through the Channel or the North Sea: shipping in the Western Approaches and the North Atlantic was open to attack on a wholly unexpected scale by the German occupation of the French Atlantic seaboard; before 1939 the Royal Navy had never even bothered to calculate the number of destroyers and other convoy escorts that would be necessary to counter such a problem. Prewar estimates of German air attack had rested on the assumption that bombers would fly from within Germany or, at worst, from the Low Countries. The fall of France made possible air attack from a wide variety of new directions, and at short range, which meant that the short- and medium-range German bombers could all reach Britain and could operate with interceptor cover for at least some of the time.

From early 1938, on the advice of Sir Thomas Inskip, the Minister for the Co-Ordination of Defence, British strategy had relied on the assumption that Britain should concentrate on mounting a defence against an attempted knock-out blow by Germany at the beginning of a war. This meant relying in the initial stages on the buildup of RAF's Fighter Command and, from early 1938, dispatching a small British Expeditionary Force across the Channel to protect Britain's first line of defence, the Low Countries and the French Channel ports. Victory was eventually to come about by the gradual development of Britain's attritional potential, subjecting Germany to a long war and to blockade which, the Great War had shown, Germany must lose.

At the time airmen had pointed to the risk that such a policy entailed. Nobody knew whether bomber attack on the scale envisaged could be resisted. Radar was in its infancy and the new generation of high-speed interceptors was only just beginning to come into production. Nobody had calculated on the fall of France, which not only made the knock-out from the air a great deal easier for the Germans to achieve, but also reversed entirely the Inskip assumption that Britain would win a long war. Now it was Britain that was likely to be starved into surrender, and not even victory in the air or resisting an invasion would take away that threat.

These huge new commitments in turn brought Britain to the verge of bankruptcy in 1940. It had always been questionable how long Inskip's 'long war' could be maintained. Britain had never fully recovered from the financial and industrial strain caused by fighting for four years in the Great War. In July 1939, the Treasury warned that planning for a three-year war was likely to be optimistic.[3] By the time of Dunkirk, such an idea was wholly unrealistic unless America lent her full weight to the struggle. The mass of weaponry lost at Dunkirk could not be replaced, and the demands of the new strategic situation could not be met, unless the Americans came in and effectively gave Britain for free the weapons with which to continue the fight. Asked to comment on the prospects for Britain if France fell, the Chiefs of Staff stated that without the full economic and financial support of the United States, 'we do not think we could continue the war with any chance of success'.[4] Those who quote Churchill's famous speech of 4 June 1940 often leave it at the phrase 'we shall never surrender', as I did in Chapter 3. What he actually continued to say was that, even if the unimaginable did happen and Britain were subjugated, the Empire would continue the fight until 'in God's good time, the new world, with all its power and might, step forth to the rescue and the liberation of the old'.[5] Even for Churchill, it seems, the real bottom line was the USA, not Britain.

It was not immediately clear that such help would be forthcoming. The USA had not always seen eye to eye with Britain over international affairs in the interwar period and, although Washington might be worried about prospects in Europe should Hitler win, it was not clear that backing Britain in what looked an almost hopeless predicament was the best investment. What if the USA gave Britain the weapons and they fell into German hands, to be used eventually against the Americans? Roosevelt's position, jockeying with isolationists in his run-up to a bid for an unprecedented third term as President, made an American decision unlikely before the election in November. If Roosevelt lost that election there would be no decision until January, when Wendell Wilkie would take over office. By August 1940 the Chancellor, Kingsley Wood, told the Cabinet that Britain's gold and dollar reserves had fallen by one-third since the beginning of the year, to £490 million. The massive new arms orders had reduced the reserves by £80 million in the past month alone and he now estimated that the remainder would last for only another three or four months.[6] At that point, unless the Americans effectively took over, Britain would have to default on her debts. Either way, Britain would be unable to carry on the war by her own efforts.

The alternatives were to surrender the future either to Germany or the United States. The first was at least discussed. In the phony war, with the occupation of Poland a *fait accompli*, some of the erstwhile appeasers were at least interested in discussing the possibility of a new general settlement – though it must include an independent Poland and Czechoslovakia in some form. It would probably be fairer to describe these notions as the development of British war aims rather than peace feelers as such, since they simply were not going to be accepted by Hitler in 1939. The moves that occurred in 1940 were originally aimed at keeping Italy out of the war during the Battle of France. Britain might have been prepared to surrender her primacy in the Mediterranean to Italy if Mussolini could have engineered a general settlement with Hitler, perhaps including the return of former German colonies. Churchill's view was that Hitler was unlikely to compromise in the middle of such a stunning military victory, and that Britain might as well fight on for at least a few more months to show that she would not be defeated. Hitler's peace terms would probably be insufferable now, he seemed to imply, so why not fight on since the invasion of Britain was a much tougher proposition than anything Hitler had yet attempted. There were further semi-formal avenues opened through Sweden in June, brought to an abrupt end by Churchill's declaration in the House of Commons that the Battle of Britain was about to begin and that the nation and the Empire should prepare for its 'finest hour'.[7]

Clive Ponting has noted that 'at the time, great secrecy naturally surrounded these discussions, but it is hard to see the justification for the later attempt to pretend that they never happened at all'.[8] On one level, this is fair comment. Ponting suggests it was a deliberate attempt to protect the heroic myth of 1940, in particular Churchill's postwar assertion that the Cabinet wasted no time on such matters as they prepared to fight on to victory, whatever the price. Perhaps all that it shows is that Churchill was not yet in a strong enough position simply to impose his views on the old heavyweights, Chamberlain and Halifax, both of whom saw the chance of getting away with at least some sort of compromise in the débâcle. Certainly, what we do know about the affair throws further bad odour on, if anyone, the 'Guilty Men' rather than the government as a whole. Churchill was supported in his stance by his new political allies, Clement Attlee of Labour and Sir Archibald Sinclair of the Liberals, but nothing was sold out anyway. Nobody came up with a list of concessions that they were prepared to lay before Hitler. Even if they had done so, the situation in Europe was such that Hitler is unlikely to have compromised with anyone. David Reynolds has pointed out that there was not much alternative to Churchillian bluff, unless one is prepared to consider the chilling though hardly credible revisionist view that peace with Hitler in 1940 would have saved Britain from the worst of what was to follow.[9] It is no real undermining of the bulldog spirit to accept that coming to terms with Hitler was considered, and then dropped. The military situation clearly warranted such discussion, certainly at a time when even Robert Menzies of Australia was ominously non-bellicose. Britain was still left to survive on her own until America made up her mind.

The Battle of Britain must be one of the very few battles to be given a name before it even began, by Churchill on 18 June. The dates for the Battle itself remain vague: the British thought they had actually been fighting it for a month before the Germans began what they saw as their concerted attempt to defeat the British fighter force, and the end of the Battle itself merged imperceptibly into the bombing of London, which had a different aim. The myth of the Battle of Britain is very different from that of the myth of Dunkirk, or the myth of the Blitz. Representations of the Battle of Britain rest on a heroic-ization of the élite fighter pilots rather than the mass of Britons, encapsulated in Churchill's paeon to 'the few'. Yet government and media at the time were anxious to point out the role played by the mass of people in the period after Dunkirk to make survival possible.

Nowhere was this more true than on the industrial front. Ernest Bevin, the new Minister of Labour, had secured the agreement of both employers and unionists for the suspension of practices that might impede production and, on 4 June, the Joint Consultative Committee, representing both sides of industry, agreed that any wage disputes which proved irreconcilable would be referred to independent arbitration, the findings of which would be binding. This led to Order 1305, which made strikes and lockouts illegal wherever collective bargaining was established, with the right of appeal to a National Arbitration Tribunal. Working days lost through stoppages fell from 1,354,000 in 1939 to 941,000 in 1940. In the metals, engineering and shipbuilding industries, stoppages were halved. While strikes were on the increase again by 1941, and higher than the 1939 level by 1942 and for the rest of the war, it is quite clear that the national emergency – in some way, and for whatever reason – struck a national chord. The hugely reassuring presence of Ernest Bevin alongside Winston Churchill in the Cabinet, so unlikely an alliance just months before, undoubtedly stood as a signifier to working-class people that times were changing. The Dunkirk spirit on the industrial front is explicable as a natural enough response both to the crisis and the new partnership of labour and capital that the government seemed to project.

The myth of 1940, as I have said before, rests on a basis of unassailable fact. Production soared in the aftermath of Dunkirk. Even so, armaments could not be produced merely by expressing the need for them. The production boom of the summer of 1940 was the result of the uphill slog in gearing British industry to potential war needs that began in the 1930s. This was particularly true in the case of the aircraft industry. The production of aircraft in Britain had already more than doubled between 1938 and 1939 before it nearly doubled again in 1940,[10] the result of crucial interventions in the traditional working of private enterprise by those such as Air Chief Marshal Sir Wilfred Freeman and Lords Weir and Swinton in the previous five years.[11] In the crucial area of fighter production, it is true, output doubled in the second quarter of 1940 and went up to 1900 in the third quarter, but this increase was at the expense of other munitions of war. Even though half a million rifles of Great War vintage crossed the Atlantic in the summer, many in the Home Guard would have had to fight the invaders with broomsticks.

Beaverbrook, as Minister for Aircraft Production, undoubtedly had the gift for publicity and for stirring national sentiments. Aircraft factories began to work for twenty-four hours a day, seven days a week. Bank holidays were cancelled. One small factory in the Midlands, which was the only source of the carburettors for the Rolls Royce Merlin engines that powered the Hurricane and the Spitfire, doubled its weekly output in a fortnight. For all that, such efforts did not make for efficiency. As the Great War had shown, a twelve-hour day did not make for greater production in the long term than a ten-hour day. Production rose by a quarter in the week after Dunkirk, but was down to the previous level four weeks later, without any decrease in working hours. Bevin ordered a limit on working hours to sixty a week, with regular rest days. Beaverbook ignored him and continued to plead for, and get, men and women to work in aircraft factories on Sundays.[12]

Bevin was the practical organizer, the negotiator who established the practical mechanics of maximum production. During the summer of 1940 he set up the complex but transparent machinery of industrial conscription, putting the case for industrial labour's involvement as a matter both of national responsibility and political opportunity. Class compromise to save the nation would give political Labour the power-sharing opportunities to improve the lives of working people:

> I have to ask you virtually to place yourself at the disposal of the State. We are Socialists, and this is the test of our Socialism. I do not want you to get worried too much about every individual that may be in the Government. We could not stop to have an election; we could not stop to decide the issue. But this I am convinced of: If our Movement and our class rise with all their energy now and save the people of this country from disaster, the country will turn with confidence forever to the people who saved them.[13]

Beaverbrook, by contrast, offered something more populist than the argument for pragmatic compromise, a depoliticized version of a People's War. The fervour he had shown in selling newspapers he now employed in involving as many as he could in the race to provide 'the few' with the fighters to defeat the Luftwaffe. He brought an unprecedented and lively razzmatazz to the business of government. On 10 July through his newspapers, he appealed for aluminium pots and pans to turn into Spitfires and Hurricanes. The Women's Voluntary Service salvage dumps were subsequently flooded with kettles, tin baths, cigarette boxes and all sorts of other household items, all of which could have produced only a small quantity of high-grade aluminium. Aluminium was not, anyway, in short supply. The Spitfire Funds similarly began as a press-inspired campaign to urge the people to contribute financially to arms production. A newspaper telephoned the Ministry of Aircraft Production to ask how much a Spitfire cost and subsequently sent the Ministry a cheque for £5000. The idea was publicized and caught on. Towns and cities all over Britain and the Empire were urged to 'buy' a Spitfire, and the BBC began giving lists of contributions at the end of its news bulletins. Individual contributions were also welcome: £1 bought the thermometer of a Merlin engine, while a schoolchild's penny could buy a rivet. Over £13 million had been contributed by April 1941, and virtually every major town in Britain had its 'own' Spitfire.[14] The sums contributed virtually nothing to the cost of armaments but were a significant means of including the 'many' with the 'few'.

Contributing your old tin bath to the drive for scrap, or contributing a shilling to a Spitfire Fund were voluntary acts of participation which, while laudable for involving the people in the fight, did not contribute substantially to Britain's physical preparation. A better indicator of the extent of public involvement in the fight to survive is that, by June 1940, after working all day, nearly 1.5 million people were giving up many of their nights and days off to the Local Defence Volunteers (LDV). Anthony Eden, Secretary of State for War, had called for the formation of such a force on radio on 14 May, when the country was not yet in any immediate danger, but the response was huge. The LDV was open to any male who was exempt, by reason of the importance of his job or medical or other reasons, from military service. Many conscientious objectors in fact found that assisting in the defence of the home country was something to which they could commit themselves.

The LDV has for so long been satirized by the *Dad's Army* image of puffed-up local dignitaries serving as officers over incompetent, ageing amateur privates that it is easy to forget just what the LDV contributed in 1940. First, it allowed real military involvement in a People's War. Though initially very poorly armed, the Home Guard – as it became known from July onwards – performed essential security jobs that would have swamped the professional army if it had had to cover them: watching for airborne landings, guarding the 5000 miles of coastline, the railways stations, essential factories, providing road-blocks, checking drivers' identification and so on. Initially, the War Office was wary about arming the people, but many rural Home Guards already had their own shotguns or rifles, and some 20,000 other weapons were handed in for Home Guard use, to supplement the half a million rifles which the USA sent for Home Guard use in the summer.

Training developed on an *ad hoc* basis, often undertaken by ex-servicemen. The most famous of these training initiatives was the school set up at Osterley Park by Tom Wintringham, ex-communist and ex-commander of the British contingent of the International Brigades in the Spanish Civil War. A number of other veterans from Spain were also instructors there, experts in guerrilla warfare, 'the military art of people's war', as it was later to be known. Initially, the school was funded by the popular left-wing weekly, *Picture Post*, and was only taken over by the War Office in October. Through the summer of 1940, Wintringham, formerly a political pariah, produced a series of articles in newspapers and magazines on how civilians could fight back against military professionals.[15]

At Osterly Park, Home Guards were taught the art of street fighting, how to make Molotov cocktails to attack tanks, how to kill motor-cyclists with trip wires. Special units were developed to undertake advanced guerrilla warfare in the event of invasion, lending some real substance to Churchill's invocation to fight them in the hills, in the fields and in the streets. Wintringham claimed that there were Army attempts to close down the school, because all the LDV should be taught was how to sit in a pillbox and shoot straight. 'The "sit in a pill-box" idea, a remnant of the Maginot Line folly not yet rooted out of the British Army, met us on other occasions. We fought it in every way we could'.[16] It may be fanciful to represent the Home Guard as a potentially radical people's army, but membership clearly gave people the nearest the British were to experience of the kind of selfless involvement that the Resistance movements in occupied Europe were to undergo. The Germans actually branded the Home Guard partisans and announced that they would be shot on capture during the invasion.[17]

The second major function of the Home Guard was a social and cultural one, rather than military, and this was to reflect a fundamental meritocracy in its organization. Most company commanders and NCOs were elected, or at least emerged from the choice of the Home Guards themselves, and were retrospectively sanctioned by the higher echelons. Many 'Colonel Blimps' emerged from the decaying wood-work to command the units but they were soon weeded out. It was a process that involved the recognition and respect for personal skills, which allowed the local poacher to have the best rifle, or the publican to be the administrative officer.

The point I am making, by concentrating on everyday life in the summer of 1940, is that the new patterns of experience forced by the danger of invasion amplified the sense of social interdependence, but also of individual capacity, of personal challenge. The experience was easy to mythicize because it was so unfamiliar, but also because it was generally so positive and involving. It virtually demanded over-arching explanation. By June 1940, the daily life of the population was as committed as it ever would be to the war. Some 17,758,000 people were working in industry, a figure to be surpassed only once during the remainder of the war, and a quarter of a million fewer than had been in civil employment a year before. The rise in the armed forces made this necessary: 2,273,000 by June 1940, compared with 480,000 a year before. Women already made up 30 per cent of the workforce, compared with 26 per cent in 1938, to rise to 39 per cent by 1944. A further 345,000 were involved in Civil Defence, the police or the fire services.[18] With the fall of France, the sole purpose of this major reorganization of the population was national survival. Nearly half the population of the East Anglian and Kentish coastal towns was moved to safer areas. From other areas, nearly a quarter of a million children took part in a second wave of evacuation, even though most soon returned to their families, preferring to be with them rather than among strangers in such a crisis.

Barricades were prepared alongside arterial roads and country lanes. The beaches of the south coast were mined and covered with barbed wire. Sports grounds and pasture land, possible landing sites for gliders or aircraft, were strewn with old motor vehicles or iron bedsteads as obstacles. Pillboxes were built around the countryside to delay the invaders' advance. Car owners were compelled to immobilize their cars when they were not in use, and road signs and place names were removed. Government instructions became specific, staccato, non-negotiable:

> What do I do? I remember that this is the moment to act like a soldier. I do not get panicky. I *stay put*. I do *not* say: 'I must get out of here'. I remember that fighting men must have clear roads. I do *not* go on to the road on bicycle, in a car or on foot. Whether I am at work or at home I just *stay put*.[19]

At the same time, measures had been taken to control the enemy within. Alien internment had begun in May and was extended to the

Italian population of less than twenty years' residence in June. Under the Treachery Act, 1600 people were held in detention without trial by August.

Britain was becoming a very unfamiliar place, turned in on itself. John Taylor has noted how a general scramble began in 1940 to record Britain in order to preserve it. The threat of invasion and mass destruction led the British to replicate themselves on paper – quite literally, on a personal level, for possible insurance purposes, but also metaphorically – to preserve a heritage. During that beautiful hot summer, following as it did the successful campaigns in the 1930s to improve access to the countryside, the people were virtually unable to visit the country or the seaside. Even if they did, there was little to see except barbed wire and pillboxes. Many of Britain's beauty spots were now restricted to military access, defence areas, and civilians needed a pass to enter. Instead, publishers remembered the countryside for them, pictorialized in a large spate of photographic essays. 'Britain' came to mean the countryside again (and, more particularly, the English countryside, as it had always threatened to do since the Romantic movement). For H.V. Morton, as for Priestley's and *Dawn Guard's* Local Defence Volunteers, heritage was threatened by the barbarians. The Central Council for the Care of Churches began a photographic record of every church in the country, and the Royal Institute of British Architects began its National Buildings Record.[20]

Like the summer of 1914, the summer of 1940 has come to represent the moment of calm before the storm. But while the summer of 1914 is projected as carefree and oblivious, the summer of 1940 is careworn and fretful. Even tea was rationed, from 9 July. A letter to the *Radio Times* pleaded for fuller focus and seriousness in dealing with the situation: 'I beseech you to cease broadcasting racing and sports news at such a time'[21]. If *Guilty Men* provided a focus for explaining how this had all came about, it was 'the top people's paper', *The Times,* ardent supporter of Chamberlain in the 1930s, which was among the first to give concrete form to what it entailed. At a time of such restriction, it was the quality press which made the point that the failures of interwar Britain had not simply been in the international sphere. If Britain was now fighting tyranny, it should also understand that there was a tyranny involved in the free market. The supposedly iron laws of economics also needed to be defeated if the fight against fascism was to make true sense. *The Times'* leader of 1 July was virtually a manifesto for reconstruction:

If we speak of freedom, we do not mean a rugged individualism which excludes social organization and economic planning. If we speak of equality, we do not mean a political equality nullified by social and economic privilege. If we speak of economic reconstruction, we think less of maximum production . . . than of equitable distribution. . . . The new order cannot be based on the preservation of privilege, whether the privilege be that of a country, of a class, or of an individual.[22]

Such sentiments were already being widely expressed privately by 'top people' such as Duff Cooper, Harold Nicolson, even Chamberlain himself in the last months of his life.[23] MO noted that the crisis had deepened popular political interest, particularly among the better off: 'it has been hard to find, even among women, many who do not unconsciously regard this war as in some way revolutionary, or radical.'[24] Even if, later in the war, MO was to find that many working-class people were cynical about the prospect of social progress, the fact that so many among the politically significant class were thinking in such a way suggests that the country was going to get social change, like it or not.

It was understandable, with the British Army virtually disarmed and the Luftwaffe just across the Channel, that Churchill had little truck with those who began to seek the immediate publication of peace aims. First, Britain had to survive, and then to win. The first of these requirements would have to occupy Britain single-mindedly for months to come. Officially in Britain, the Battle of Britain is dated from 10 July, but the Luftwaffe had already started to attack convoys in the Channel, at great cost to themselves. At this point, the plans for the invasion of Britain were not too far advanced. Like the evacuation from Dunkirk, the Battle of Britain was an event in which only a minority actually participated directly. While people on the ground could watch the dog-fights over Kent and London, they could have had no idea what was really happening. For those living north of London the media were their only eyes and ears on the conflict, their only access to 'the truth'. Not only what was happening but how it was reported became crucial aspects of the construction of the longest and the biggest battle ever fought on British soil. In the early air fighting, the BBC settled on a style of reportage that was akin to sports commentary: 'the man's baled out by parachute – the pilot's baled out by parachute – he's a Junkers 87 and he's going slap into the sea and there he goes – smash. . . . Oh boy, I've never seen anything so good as this – the RAF fighters have really got these boys taped.'[25]

The Air Ministry encouraged this style of spreading information with their habit of summarizing the day's operations in the form of relative losses, like scores in a football match. Newspaper vendors chalked up such legends as 'Biggest raid ever – Score 78 to 26 – England still batting'.[26] It is symptomatic of the faith which the BBC and the M.o.I. were learning to put in the people that they often issued the Luftwaffe claims alongside those of the Air Ministry without any really disparaging comment. On 8 August, for example, the BBC reported that the Air Ministry claimed sixty kills for the loss of twenty British fighters, while the Luftwaffe claimed forty-nine kills for the loss of thirty-one. In fact, both sides consistently overestimated the damage they had caused to the other side. There may well have been some deliberate over-egging of the figures, but it is extremely difficult to estimate enemy kills from pilots' reports of confused skirmishes fought at great speed in three dimensions. Even now, the true figures of losses in the Battle remain a matter of some dispute. In the 1969 film *The Battle of Britain*, Lawrence Olivier's Dowding, when asked whether the British claims were genuine, replied with quiet exasperation: 'I'm not interested in propaganda. If we're right, they'll give up. If we're wrong, they'll be in London in a week.'[27]

For the Germans, the Battle proper did not begin until mid-August.[28] On 12 August, an attack was made on the radar chain and on the fighter aerodromes as a preliminary to *Adlertag* the following day. The plan was to destroy Fighter Command within a month so as to make invasion possible. The Luftwaffe launched its maximum effort on 15 August, attacking simultaneously from Norway as well as from across the Channel. The attack from Norway was disastrous for the Germans as they had no fighter cover but, further south, London experienced its first major taste of bombing. The RAF claimed to have shot down 182 aircraft that day, for the loss of thirty-four fighters. Similarly overwrought claims were made in the ensuing days. A heavily outnumbered but technically superb force, it seemed, was at least keeping at bay the force that had shattered Belgium, Holland and France in seven weeks. On 20 August Churchill told the House of Commons: 'never in the field of human conflict was so much owed by so many to so few.'

Cinema newsreels were not quite so immediate in their impact as radio, of course, but they could be produced within three or four days. For obvious reasons, much of the aerial footage which the newsreels used in 1940 was from the archives. They tended to concentrate on the happy camaraderie of young men on the ground, smoking their pipes, petting their dogs and playing cricket in full flying kit waiting

Figure 5 First of the Few, 1942. A low-key Leslie Howard dreams the evolution of the Spitfire but dies before his offspring saves England. The Hurricane was the work-horse of the Battle of Britain, but the Spitfire was the more dashing, technologically advanced charger for the the Knights of the Air. © Carlton, courtesy of the British Film Institute.

to scramble, or returning to give their reports of the hunt. It was clearly difficult to resist the sporting and chivalric metaphor when dealing with this new breed of hero, the fighter pilot, the new knight errant of a technological age. Their individualism, their control of an awesomely fast, extraordinarily manoeuvrable machine, the way they drew vapour trails across the sky as they dived in to attack the plodding, methodical banks of bombers appeared to reinvest warfare with some sense of grace. There was no hint in the newsreels of the cacophony of the fighter's war, the brain-numbing sound of engine manifolds at ear height on either side of the cramped cockpit, no hint of the frustration of so often failing to find the enemy or, on finding him, having the guns jam after a couple of seconds.[29]

Significantly, it was the Spitfire fighter which was to occupy the centre of public attention, even though there were many more Hurricanes involved in the Battle, and even though the Hurricanes did most of the donkey work against the bombers. The elegance of the Spitfire design, the story of the designer who had fought to have it accepted but had not lived to see it in operation, was to be the subject of the first major film about the Battle, *First of the Few*, which appeared early in 1942. In this construction, Spitfire pilots were depicted as untroubled by being outnumbered: 'six to one – piece of cake', and after a dog-fight the hero drew back his cockpit canopy to look at the sky and pay tribute to the dead designer: 'Mitch, they can't take the Spitfire. Mitch, they just can't take 'em'.[30] The film's theme was individualism faced with mindless mass organization: R.J. Mitchell's struggle with the bureaucrats to get his design accepted and the fighter pilots' struggle with the massed array of similarly faceless bombers. As the Battle began to be mythologized after it was over, the individualism of the fighter pilots and the superiority of the Spitfire began to be high-lighted, as against the team effort and the complicated interrelated technology that had actually won the day.

At the risk of being accused of the kind of counter-factual argument of which I have accused others, it is worth putting the Battle in its strategic context, because it has become such a significant element in projecting 1940 as a victory. Fighter Command was not in fact all that heavily outnumbered and enjoyed several important strategic advantages, which offset the numerical disparity. Fighter Command had 666 aircraft in the front line at the beginning of the Battle, with about 750 in reserve. Production had reached the stage at which, for most of the Battle, there were enough replacements available to maintain front line strength. The Luftwaffe had 700 single-seat fighters, which were technically a match for the British but could only operate for short periods over British airspace because of their limited range. The 260 two-seat fighters and 300 dive-bombers the Germans had available proved too cumbersome to be more than a liability against Spitfires. The Luftwaffe had 1000 bombers but they had been designed primarily for army support, and lacked the bomb load to do decisive damage against such an extended target system as that presented by Fighter Command. Neither could German aircraft production keep up with the pace of Luftwaffe losses during the Battle, priority having been switched to other armaments. Though Fighter Command suffered a critical shortage of pilots as the Battle continued, the Luftwaffe's losses were to be even more critical because every pilot shot down over Britain was either killed or captured. If a British pilot survived he could be back with his squadron within days. Most critical of all, the Luftwaffe failed to understand the central importance of radar to Fighter Command's strategy. One radar station was put out of action for ten days, at Ventnor in the Isle of Wight, but the rest of the chain continued to provide Air Chief Marshal Dowding with the intelligence that allowed him to commit his forces in the most economical way.

When he gave Fighter Command his famous valediction, Churchill could not know that the worst was yet to come. On 24 August the Luftwaffe began more dangerous tactics, concentrating on the sector airfields in the South of England which were vital to Fighter Command's organization and to the whole strategy of preventing invasion. A critical fortnight followed, in which Fighter Command almost lost the Battle. Six of the seven most important sector stations became almost inoperable and, in those two weeks, Fighter Command lost over 20 per cent of its front-line pilots. But German tactics changed again. Apparently believing that Fighter Command was on the point of collapse, Hitler sanctioned the bombing of London, partly as a reprisal for British attacks on Berlin, partly in the hope that the Luftwaffe could lure the remaining British fighters into a desperate, losing battle to save their capital. On 7 September a large force of bombers began to attack the East End of London at about 5 p.m., and subsequent waves of bombers continued the attack until 4.30 the next morning. The fires that started could be seen over thirty miles away, and 430 Londoners died that night with over 400 more the following night. The Luftwaffe was to return to the capital for seventy-four out of the subsequent seventy-five nights.

The Battle of Britain had moved seamlessly into the Blitz. When the Battle of London started, pressure was taken off the grievously pressed Fighter Command organization. The codeword Cromwell, which meant 'invasion imminent', was issued on the eve of the first major attack on London and remained in force for almost two weeks. In fact, Hitler had postponed the invasion until 21 September. Yet one more big raid was planned for 15 September to test the remaining strength of Fighter Command. Given more time than normal because of the lack of the usual diversionary attacks to split the defence, Dowding was able to send in the big wing of linked squadrons to hit the bombers in numbers. The BBC claimed 185 German aircraft shot down. Again, it was a major overstatement, but it must have been clear to Hitler that Fighter Command simply was not on the verge of defeat. Meanwhile, a decision on invasion could not be avoided for much longer, as RAF's Bomber Command began to hit the vulnerable barges and other craft assembling in the Dutch ports. On 17 September the invasion was postponed indefinitely. Ten days later, Hitler ordered preparations for the invasion of the Soviet Union.[31] Nobody in Britain knew it, but the Battle of Britain had in effect been won. London and the other cities of Britain would continue to be softened up to weaken still further the ability of the nation to retaliate – by night from October onwards, so that they became virtually invulnerable to the RAF's fighters – but there would be no invasion.

Since the war, it has become less clear that the Germans were ever wholly serious about an invasion of Britain. From Gordon Wright in the 1960s through to Peter Calvocoressi and Guy Wint in the 1980s, it was pointed out that Hitler's directive for Operation Sealion was, at best, only half-hearted:[32] it was an order 'to prepare for and, *if neces-sary*, carry out'[33] such an invasion, a directive wholly different in tone from those which preceded the invasions of France or the Soviet Union. Perhaps Hitler was aware of just how risky such an operation would be. Even if Fighter Command were defeated, there would still be all the risks of an opposed sea crossing, and the constant problem of keeping open the lines of communication against the attacks of the Royal Navy. If Hitler's major aim in life was to achieve *lebensraum* in Eastern Europe, there was not much point in such an operation. Recently, a German scholar has even claimed that the Battle of Britain was simply a feint to cover preparations for Operation Barbarossa against the Soviet Union.[34]

It is at least credible to argue that with France gone and Britain seriously weakened, there was no great risk in leaving Britain bloodied but unbowed in the West. Even if the Americans came in, it would be years before a real threat could develop from that quarter again, by which time the apocalyptic battle in the East should have been won, and there would be little the West could do about it.[35] The front that the British opened in North Africa and the Mediterranean hardly seems to have impinged on the Germans: Rommel was able to keep them at bay for a considerable period on a military shoestring. The RAF's strategic air offensive on Germany began to have serious effects only relatively late in the war. It was not until the invasion of France in 1944 that the long-term significance of British survival in 1940 became clear, that the islands could be used as a stepping-stone by the United States. But if the Soviet Union had not survived and then began to drive the Germans into the dust, it is not clear whether even that would have been possible. On balance, if the defeat of Fighter Command had been assured, Hitler would have been more tempted than he was to invade. As it was, it seems that he took the calculated risk to leave Britain to wither on the vine, and to proceed with the attack in the East which would have established a virtually impregnable domination of Europe.

Such a perspective does not wholly diminish Britain and the way that she fought back in 1940. How one interprets what happened depends, literally, on where one stands in the world. For Britain and the British, it was clearly a victory, because defeat would have had appalling and probably irreversible consequences. For the United States, too, it was eventually a kind of victory, 'the pivotal event of the war',[36] the key strategic event which gave the Americans a chance to intervene directly in Europe when they finally chose to do so. For the Germans, it rankled as a setback in the war and, certainly during the cold war years, it may have suited West Germans to salute the strength of their new allies, but the Battle of Britain was hardly a decisive event compared with what was to happen in the Soviet Union. In the official Soviet history of the war, the Battle of Britain rated only a footnote. In Japan, the Battle appears to have been viewed as a stalemated postscript to the Battle of France, which did nothing to undermine the decision to exploit the weakness of all the European imperial powers in the Far East.

The myth of the Battle of Britain, like that of Dunkirk, is not an international myth. Although both have some credence in America, they are culturally specific. They speak of a particular national crisis, and they represent only one corner of the overall landscape of 1940 in international terms. They are also at odds with one another. While Dunkirk and the Dunkirk spirit speak of the mass of British people overcoming the mistakes of the past, of a people finding themselves again, the Battle of Britain came to speak of a gallant few who had held the enemy at bay and thus protected the many. Priestley, as usual, managed to find a question to ask about all this: What would happen to them after the war? Would they, like the heroes of the Great War, reappear a few years later as 'shabby, young-oldish men' selling second-hand cars or office equipment, or trailing around the suburbs trying to sell vacuum cleaners?[37] During the following months, however, the focus returned once more to the many, as British cities experienced the greatest fear of the interwar years about the next war, the mass bombing of the civilian population. If the 'People's War' was a victory, a domestic victory over the legacy of the 1930s in Britain as well as over the Luftwaffe, it was purely defensive, a social rather than an international victory. It was to be in the way that the moral authority of Britain in the Blitz was to be translated into international currency by British politicians after the war that many of Britain's later international problems were to become institutionalized.

5   The Blitz

A major problem with living through the Blitz was that it was quite indiscriminate. You could not avoid death simply because you were not in uniform. Someone you could not see and who could not see you could kill you in your own home. Once again, it was the extraordinariness and the incongruity of everyday life that needed explanation. The impact of bombing was never as apocalyptic as had been expected before the war, but it would be simplistic as well as patronizing to those who lived through it to minimize its impact. This style of warfare was utterly indiscriminate; it killed Old Age Pensioners and babies, middle class and working class, even the odd aristocrat. Some 3500 British soldiers had been killed in the Battle of France. Over 40,000 civilians were killed between September 1940 and May 1941, and it was not until late 1942 that total British uniformed casualties in the war exceeded civilian. This was, in the most literal sense, a people's war. Bombing targeted the economic, social and cultural fabric of the nation, and in so doing it laid bare the sinews that articulated the nation, exposing them to close examination.

Although we can pinpoint precisely the naming of the Battle of Britain – it was Churchill's phrase – this is much more difficult both with the 'People's War' and with the 'Blitz'. The first was widely in use by the end of 1940 but, as a phrase, it goes back at least as far as the Spanish Civil War, and it has specifically Marxist roots as a concept. Its entrée into mainstream British usage is probably through veterans of the Spanish Civil War such as Tom Wintringham, though its political potency was rapidly diluted as it became popular. In one sense, it simply meant that a lot more people were fighting this war than were in uniform, and its implications were widely different depending on who was using the phrase. 'Blitz' was a shortening of 'blitzkrieg', which had been used by the international press as shorthand to describe the lightning speed of the new methods of war that the *Wehrmacht* employed in Poland in September 1939. But the shortened form, 'blitz', is really only ever used to describe the bombing of British cities in 1940–41. It is interesting that the British prefer to use a German word for such a 'German' act, as if there could not be an English word to cover the stunning and brutal destructive power of air attack. Air war is total war *par excellence* and even with the development of more precise weapons technology in recent air wars, it is widely accepted that there will be collateral damage, that hospitals will be bombed and children killed. The difference in the British projection of 1940 is that collateral damage was projected not as an unavoidable side-effect but as a deliberate act of the Germans. In the wake of the attack on Coventry on 14 November, the *Daily Herald* proclaimed the bombing as the foulest deed that even Hitler had ordained: 'Have no scruples about military objectives. Kill men, kill women, kill children. Destroy! Destroy! Destroy! Heil Hitler! Heil bloodshed! Heil pain!' In building the myth of the Blitz, commentators insisted on the 'calm courage of ordinary British people in this hell of Hitler's making'.[1] Many also insisted on something more; that the implications of this mass destruction were to create both the opportunities and the demands for large-scale social reconstruction. A people repairing the breaches in the national walls left by the Guilty Men would not allow the world of the 1930s to be rebuilt.

There was much less need for propaganda than had been expected, and even less need for social policing. That the danger of air attack had been exaggerated before the war made the reality that much easier to take. There were differences of opinion on how much morale was affected. MO tended to be more pessimistic in its reflections on morale than Home Intelligence, for example. Descriptions of the state of morale partly depended on preformed assumptions. MO, consciously or unconsciously, may have had motives for expecting morale to crack (that assumption of a gap between governors and governed on which MO had been founded) and this may have coloured their researches. Home Intelligence issued daily reports on morale through the summer of 1940 but switched to weekly reports in October, when it became clear to them that there was no immediate danger that the public would collapse. They realized fairly quickly that morale did not depend on the shock caused by single raids but on longer-term issues. It did not matter very much to the war effort anyway if people were worried or nervous of air attacks, as long as they got on with their lives and their jobs. Prewar assumptions that a breakdown in morale would lead to mass panic and riot were simply unfounded. There may have been local and temporary 'passive' breakdowns in morale, with people feeling nervous and cynical about the outcome of the war. There is the suggestion that defeatist slogans appeared on walls in some blitzed cities, but there was never any sign of an 'active' breakdown in morale.[2]

Even without exhortation or promises for the future, it was clear that elemental issues were at stake. Too much was destroyed and too much threatened to make it possible to contemplate a return to the old ways of life. The fact that children were potential targets itself raised the most critical issues about the regeneration of society itself. Richard Titmuss, in 1950, suggested that the conditions of 1940 provided a permanent basis for the creation of the welfare state in the postwar period, and that what happened to children during the war was a litmus test of prewar assumptions about social policy.[3] Recently, Titmuss' analysis has come under threat from those who believe that he exaggerated the national unity engendered by the war and that he thus contributed to the rosy, comfortable picture of a nation reborn in crisis. Yet the fact remains that evacuation was a huge social experiment and that, even if most evacuees returned to their homes fairly quickly, it did have the effect of showing one side of the nation to the other. This did not always have beneficial effects: often quite the reverse. In the case of the first evacuation, which began on 1 September 1939, the intention was to get the children out of the urban centres as soon as possible, in case the war began with an attempted knock-out blow. About 1.5 million people were voluntarily moved, far fewer than had been expected by a government foreseeing a panic flight from the cities which might have to be fiercely policed.

Although the evacuation from the cities proceeded relatively smoothly, there were major problems in the reception areas, where planning was much less well founded. There were serious mismatches between evacuees and their foster-parents – religious, social and cultural problems. But it was not the luckless evacuees who received media sympathy on the whole, but the reception areas. Stories abounded in many uncomprehending and disapproving middle-class reception areas of dirty, ill-mannered children and their feckless mothers out for what they could get in the new and often very much more prosperous environment in which they found themselves.[4] It was probably the mismatches as much as the fact that the knock-out blow attempt did not initially materialize that caused so many of the evacuees to return home: by February 1940, 44 per cent of school-children and 87 per cent of mothers and preschool children had gone back. However, a second evacuation began in the summer of 1940 and developed still further as the bombing began of cities not previously expected to be serious targets. By February 1941, the official evacuee population stood at 1,370,000 and had only declined to 1,205,000 by September.[5] This was, by any measure, a truly major social upheaval.[6]

Certainly a shock was registered among the intelligentsia about the poverty of many of the urban working class. Richard Padley and Margaret Cole, in their survey of evacuation for the Fabians in 1940, highlighted fairly simple and basic problems of clothing, health and educational standards, as did surveys by Alfred Body and MO.[7] These surveys showed that the underclass of the interwar years remained the underclass. Seebohm Rowntree's study of working-class life in York in the mid-1930s appeared in 1940 as well, and there can be little doubt that his conclusions and suggestions registered even more strongly with the political class for the context of the Blitz. Some reactions to the shock were as hostile as many of those from the reception areas. Much of the research reported by the Women's Group on Public Welfare, *Our Towns*, which appeared in 1942, suggested that many of the problems revealed by the evacuees were endemic to a lumpenproletariat of socially inadequate people.[8]

Whatever the opinion as to their cause, the point is that evacuation suggested that working-class children had significant problems, under-lined by social concerns over the 36 per cent rise in indictable offences by juveniles in 1940, with particularly notable increases in larceny and breaking and entering.[9] By the end of 1940, the inadequacies of local authorities in dealing with reception of evacuees began to be ironed out as central government made more money available for social clubs and welfare centres. So, as the threat from the bombers to the cities continued and the remaining evacuees settled down to life in the country, evacuation became one small but significant means of dealing with social casualties. This was not so much because there had been a revolution in social awareness; it was because a problem accepted as virtually endemic in poor urban areas had been transferred to areas where it was not acceptable. The focus of analysis had switched from an understanding that the poor were always with us to a realiza-tion that they were actually living in our houses, no longer safely ghettoized in 'distressed areas'.

Medical and other social services were made aware of the particular problems caused to children not only by evacuation but also for those who remained in the cities. To be blamelessly at risk from urban squalor was one thing; to be blamelessly at risk from being killed by a bomb was quite another. Psychiatrists claimed that children were much more likely to suffer psychological disturbance in bombing than adults. That was harrowing to endure. Other changes were equally destabilizing for children and young people. About 20 per cent of the nation's schools were to be damaged by bombing, and many others were converted into rest centres to deal with those made homeless. Absenteeism rose alarmingly. Teachers were swapped around from school to school or sent to evacuation centres. By the end of 1941, the effects were becoming clear: in West Ham, in one elementary school, it was found that not a single seven-year-old could read.[10]

There was some considerable hostile reaction to the way the rich could buy their children a more comfortable sort of disruption. Urban public schools moved lock, stock and barrel to safer quarters; Duff Cooper sent his son to Canada, Mountbatten sent his family to the United States, followed by the well-heeled young Jeremy Thorpe and Vera Brittain's daughter, the future Shirley Williams. The class friction that Home Intelligence noticed on this issue was an understandable reaction to a situation in which a rich few could buy themselves not just a better life, which had always been true, but even their personal safety in a national emergency.[11] These details of everyday life clicked easily into the overarching explanations of what was going on provided by those such as Priestley on radio.

In dealing with the evacuees and the disruption of schooling, teachers, educationalists, paediatricians, billeting officers, parents and foster-parents – a huge range of people – became aware of a major social problem brewing which would fundamentally affect the next generation: this was the basic fact of their everyday life. If children appeared to be going backwards, that was just one of the myriad worrying problems which emerged from the huge social disruption caused by the Blitz. London, in the long, nightly siege through the autumn and winter of 1940–41, may or may not have come near to breakdown on a number of occasions, depending on where one throws the light. Home Intelligence reported nervous tension building in the capital long before the first raids but, by September, it was reporting that morale remained relatively high, apart from small groups of individuals. MO, on the other hand, felt that morale was at best flimsy. Comments such as 'we didn't ask for this blinking war, did we?' prompted Negley Farson to comment, 'these people are beginning to lose faith – faith in all degrees of people higher up'.[12] While the Luftwaffe was able to concentrate its firepower on the East End, there was always the danger that class friction might turn into open warfare. In Stepney, where the first big raid was centred on 7 September, 200,000 people lived twelve to a building in Victorian slum tenements that crumpled and burned furiously with the bombs.

Houses that had been condemned as unsuitable for habitation for years just collapsed. It was here that communists and blackshirts had clashed in the 1930s, and the borough contained just the sort of racial mix that prewar pessimists had assumed would be ripe for panic and riot under attack.

Certainly, there were those in the centre of things who were fearful. Harold Nicolson, at the M.o.I., felt that 'everybody is worried about the feeling in the East End. . . . There is much bitterness. It is said that even the King and Queen were booed the other day when they visited the destroyed areas',[13] an interesting, rather patrician comment on the supposed role of the Royal Family as guarantors of national unity. The story may or may not have been true – rumours were rife among the political caste as well as in the streets and pubs – but the Queen was later famously to say that she was glad when Buckingham Palace was bombed on 13 September, because it meant she could look the East End in the face again. The real danger, however, was not the direct effect of the bombers themselves but the fact that Britain had made the wrong arrangements for coping with the effects on the ground. There was reported to be particular anger over the lack of post-raid organization. Prewar preparations had been made on the assumption that there would be thousands of fatal casualties. What they had not reckoned with was the large numbers left alive but homeless. Neither were there enough public shelters. The freely issued Anderson shelters were of no use in an area where there were so few gardens. The situation was only remedied when people took the law into their own hands and occupied the underground railway system and the Tilbury railway arches. The authorities acquiesced, but new problems were created.

Commentators weaved together somewhat nervous-sounding assertions that the victims were courageous and stoical, with warnings about the possible consequences if they were not. The *Manchester Guardian* summoned the names of Cobbett and Booth to describe the 'spirit of chivalry [which] has inspired numberless scenes of mutual aid and brave unselfishness into this atmosphere of ruin and danger'. But the problems of the homeless raised a major question of national responsibility:

> The losses of East London are a national liability. Those who have suffered must be regarded not as victims of misfortune, whose adversities are to be tempered by charity, but as citizens who happen to have received blows from the common enemy which other citizens have so far escaped. The perspective is important,

for nothing would do more to undermine the spirit of solidarity in the nation than a failure of imagination in treating this problem. The other night some fifty persons from the East End took refuge in the shelter of the Savoy Hotel and refused to leave. This is a symptom.[14]

Many of the well-to-do certainly continued to live well in West London through the Blitz. The diaries of John Colville and Harold Nicolson seem to show no dampening of the social whirl, busy though both men were supposed to be with the running of the war. The incident to which the *Guardian* was referring was the occupation by East End communists of the restaurant dormitory in the underground banqueting hall in the Savoy on 15 September. In fact, the event appears to have passed relatively quietly, but it did focus on the fact that, in the early days of the Blitz, the rich seemed to be getting off relatively lightly. Paradoxically, partly through guilt perhaps, it was the mouthpiece of the well-to-do which reacted with the most progressive constructions of what would have to be done. Commenting on the setting up of a new Ministry of Works and Buildings in October, *The Times* took a longer view on the possibilities:

Rebuilding there will have to be after the war, and much new building: but the reconstruction . . . does not begin with building, nor does it end there. The reconstruction of England will reshape many ways of life and will attack poverty and slumdom, ignorance and ill health, the insecurities of employment, the closed doors of opportunity. Indeed a solid, stable and not slow social reconstruction, and some considerable industrial reconstruction, will be the task of reformers after the war – nothing less than a replanning of the national life.[15]

Part of the worry of *The Times*, no doubt, was that unless the masses were given social change they would simply make it for themselves. There was a self-interest in the newspaper's philanthropy, and at least a hint of the old Victorian arguments for public health legislation in their appeal for better medical conditions in the shelters, that working-class diseases could easily become middle-class diseases.[16] It is significant that there was very little talk of reconstruction in the more popular dailies, where complaints tended to feature shorter-term worries, such as home insurance, post-raid rest centres, roof repairs, and the failure of the anti-aircraft batteries to put up a better show.

There was very little that the anti-aircraft guns, or the RAF, could do against bombers attacking by night. General Pile did order his gunners to put up the biggest barrage possible, more to encourage the local population than in the expectation of shooting down bombers, though it did at least force the Luftwaffe to fly higher and thus bomb more indiscriminately. It may well be that falling shell splinters were as great a threat to civilians as bombs. In London, the signs of worry that MO at least noted after the first few raids gave way to a sort of resignation as people simply got used to the Blitz. By November, a shelter census showed that only 40 per cent of central Londoners were sleeping in shelters. The rest were either at work or asleep in their homes.[17] Whatever class frictions there may have been lessened, even MO agreed, as bombs began to fall indiscriminately over the better-off parts of London as well as the East End. Thousands trekked out of London every night, rather to get a good night's sleep than in terror, as some worried observers assumed, and returned the following day to get to work.

London was simply too big a target to be hit decisively by a medium bomber force. The railway termini were often out of service, buses had to follow a circuitous route to avoid demolished streets or unexploded bombs, and gas, electricity and telephone services failed frequently, often for days at a time. On top of all the dangers to life and limb, there was the extraordinary inconvenience of life in the Blitz; yet for all that, people rarely missed going to work if it could be avoided. Partly, this may have been a response to the 1930s, the work ethic enforced by the danger of unemployment. Partly, too, it was to reassure friends and workmates that you were still alive. Partly it was the need to maintain a pattern in daily life, the same reason why most families preferred their children to be with them in the Blitz rather than in the countryside. The Ministry of Home Security reckoned that, even when a worker had lost his or her home, absence from work lasted on average for only six days.[18]

Lack of sleep proved a major difficulty for most Londoners. Even in the deep shelters you could feel the vibration of the bombs and the artillery through the walls. Bleary-eyed most of the time, civilians learned to do what soldiers did: catch five minutes' sleep whenever it was possible. Even more sleepless was the army of civil defence workers, air-raid wardens and firemen, who were stretched to the limit and sometimes beyond throughout the Blitz. Earlier in the war, the public had looked askance at the typical air-raid warden as an officious 'little Hitler', with his ubiquitous shout, 'put that light out!' In the Blitz, however, commentators allowed them to acquire respect.

Predominantly part-timers, predominantly middle-aged or elderly, their knowledge of the local community, its people and its geography was vital in inspiring confidence as well as in directing the rescue services. When the Tilbury railway shelter suffered a direct hit, it was reported that 'a single warden, standing at the top of a narrow passage, was able to control about three thousand people, who calmly and coolly groped their way through the darkness exactly as he ordered'.[19]

The Heavy Rescue squads, mostly from the peacetime building trades, used their vital civil engineering knowledge to deal with those trapped in fallen buildings, threatened not simply with the masonry but by broken gas mains and bare electrical wires. For all the hideous work they had to do in fetching out bodies, the job could bring its own reward: it was not an uncommon event to rescue a twelve year-old girl from a wrecked house after four and a half days through a thirty-foot tunnel.[20] So many of the diaries and other contemporary accounts of the Blitz also pay tribute to the work of the Auxiliary Fire Service, particularly in the great fire raids of 7 September and 29 December. In the latter raid, 1500 separate fires were started in the City with the Thames at its lowest ebb. *Picture Post*'s image of a fireman alone, high up on his ladder, playing his hose on the fire with smoke and sparks flying around him, became one of the most abiding symbols of working-class heroism in the Blitz, as totemic in its way as the same journal's photographs of unemployment in the 1930s – and the contrast between the two, of course, still helps to tell the story of how Britain 'found herself' again in 1940.[21]

The fire service of 1940 was celebrated most profoundly in Humphrey Jennings' masterly and emotive feature-length documentary *Fires Were Started*, which appeared in 1942. What singles out most of the full-length wartime documentaries from the fodder on which audiences had been fed in the 1930s, and even from many of the exhortational shorts of the war years, is their abandonment of any patronizing of the working class. Real firemen played all the characters in *Fires Were Started*. We are aware that the newcomer, Barrett, is middle-class, but he is fully accepted and pointed in the right direction by the working-class community. The film takes us through a working day in the fire service in 1940. It has a strong narrative drive, culminating in a major fire in a riverside warehouse, which threatens a ship laden with munitions lying alongside it. All night the firemen struggle to save the ship, but one of them, Jacko, is killed before the ship sails away. There follows an expert narrative closure, with the team, now seen individually, returning exhausted and silent to their posts, followed by the funeral. The title would have been

Figure 6 Picture Post 1 February 1941. Bert Hardy, the most consistently inspired of *Picture Post*'s brilliant photographers, took a series of shots of fire-fighters caught in the apocalyptic setting of the night-time Blitz. They appeared as a feature in the magazine in early 1941. © Hulton Archive.

familiar to wartime audiences as a common phrase in 1940 news bulletins, and indeed is 'refamiliarized' in the BBC broadcast which overlays the final sequence. Particularly remarkable is the absence of any need to pontificate on the war or on its implications. No bombers are seen, no one curses the Nazis, no one emphasizes the courage of the firemen in the face of such great danger. It is a sign of very effective propaganda that such things do not need to be said; by 1942, this film assumes, such notions had become established truths in the realm of common sense.[22]

'Nothing was more surreal than the Blitz', Humphrey Jennings once commented. Even more than cinema, wartime photography thrived on incongruity. Like the image of the little boats at Dunkirk, it is the incongruity, the surreal quality of photographs from the Blitz which invests that experience with meaning and emotion. A familiar London Transport bus crashed into the crater made by the bomb which hit Balham tube station, the wall of a suburban house destroyed to reveal wallpaper and furnishings which the owners would have shrunk from revealing to their neighbours in prewar days, freeze the historical process as a catastrophic inversion of the peacetime world. But it was fire which contributed the apocalyptic element to the Blitz.

The Blitz was apparently beautiful as well as tragic. A.P. Herbert, commanding a motorboat in the Thames Auxiliary Patrol on 7 September, remembered the stupendous spectacle of half a mile or more of the Surrey Docks ablaze, where 250 acres of timber had been set alight: 'The wind was westerly and the accumulated smoke and sparks of all the fires swept in a high wall across the river . . . like a lake in hell'.[23] The BBC commentator, speaking live to his audience from the roof of Broadcasting House on the same night, described how

> if this weren't so appalling, it would be one of the most wonderful sights I've ever seen. . . . And I think the most beautiful sight of all, apart from the tragedy of it, are the towers and the suspension bridge of the Tower Bridge. . . . The flames are leaping up in the air now. St Paul's, the dome of St Paul's Cathedral, is silhouetted blackly against it. . . . The smoke is going up very slowly now and it's just illuminated faintly. It's almost like the Day of Judgement as pictured in some of the old books.[24]

The raid on the City of London on 29 December gave rise to 'War's greatest picture', H.A. Mason's shot of the dome of St Paul's Cathedral

Figure 7 'War's greatest picture', *Daily Mail*, front page, 29 December 1940. What became one of the most published of all the images of the Blitz was another quite conscious moment of myth-making. The story of how the photographer waited for the right moment to click the shutter was itself part of the *Mail*'s coverage of the Blitz that day. © *Daily Mail*, 1940; photograph, Alistair Daniel.

surrounded by a sea of fire and smoke, yet itself unharmed. Unusually, the *Mail* allowed Mason to describe how he took it, so that the photograph is an admitted 'construction':

> I focused at intervals as the great dome loomed up through the smoke. Glares of many fires and sweeping clouds of smoke kept hiding the shape. Then a wind sprang up. Suddenly, the shining cross, dome and towers stood out like a symbol in the inferno. The scene was unbelievable. In that moment or two I released my shutter.

'That moment or two', a simply fortuitous combination of weather, timing and photographic instinct, published in the last days of that momentous year, came to stand as prime signifier for the Blitz as a whole.

On an inside page of the same issue, the *Daily Mail*'s reporter described the extraordinary grandeur of the scene as he walked through the City:

> Here was a sight at which to marvel. Fire blazed all around, flames dangerously close.
>
> The cathedral itself, its cross above the dome, calm and aloof above a sea of fire, stood out an island of God, safe and untouched.
>
> On, and deeper into the city. Fires, always fires: to the left, to the right, before and behind. . . .
>
> Everywhere great armies of firemen, professional and amateur, worked grimly on, too absorbed in their own fierce business to worry about the danger to fools like myself, drawn to this scene of destruction by an instinct too deep to be denied.[25]

Such events were only too easy to mythologize. They fitted with the Judaeo-Christian concepts of judgement, redemption and rebirth. While St Paul's survived, nineteen Wren churches were destroyed in London, ten in one night. Every Londoner knew they had symbolized the rebuilding of London after the Great Fire. By the same token, the four out of every ten houses destroyed or damaged in Stepney by the end of the year signified the need for another great rebuild.

The Crown Film Unit responded quickly to the London Blitz but was careful in its targeting. *London Can Take It* was aimed at the Americans, emphasizing Britain's role in holding the line for democracy. It was showing in America by mid-October. A much shorter version, renamed *Britain Can Take It*, to allay provincial sniffiness at

Figure 8 London Can Take It, 1940. 'London looks up towards the dawn.' Made primarily for an American audience to stress that the conflict was a 'People's War', this film was then released in Britain as the apparently neutral reflections of an American journalist working in London. © Imperial War Museum.

the publicity constantly given to the capital, was released free from the M.o.I. for domestic audiences. The film's subtlety as an act of persuasion, for audiences at home, was that it appeared to be a neutral foreigner's assessment of extraordinary heroism among working-class Londoners. Directed by Harry Watt and Humphrey Jennings, the film purported to be the American correspondent Quentin Reynolds' report home on one night in the London Blitz. 'This is the London rush hour. Many of the people at whom you are looking now are members of the greatest civilian army ever to be assembled. . . . Brokers, clerks, pedlars, merchants by day – they are heroes by night.' The images over which Reynolds speaks are of shelterers in the tube stations, civil defence workers, trains moving over dangerously under-mined bridges. The King and the Queen appear among the rubble of London at one point; significantly, the fact that they are on screen is not picked up in the commentary, as if they were just two more Londoners. 'A bomb has its limitations', Reynolds concludes, 'It can only destroy buildings and kill people. It cannot kill the unconquerable spirit and courage of the people of London. London can take it!' Though there are strong hints that 'England is not taking her beating lying down', that the RAF is giving it back in raids over Germany, the overall emphasis is on the passive defence of London, the response of a 'people's army', and the promise that the dawn will come: 'The sign of a great fighter in the ring is "Can he get up from the floor after being knocked down?" London does this every morning.'[26]

The film lacks the subtlety of the more mature work that Jennings was capable of producing within a couple of years, but it marked a very significant shift in the imaging of ordinary people. While *Dawn Guard* had suffered from the fake country accents of its two Home Guards, even Priestley spoke rather too cosily about 'ordinary, decent folk'. The 'Jennings Touch', as it began to emerge in this film, was to observe ordinary people in a montage of images, both as individuals and a collectivity, while the grandeur of events in which they were embroiled invested them with a heroism, through no fault nor wish of their own.

While London got used to the Blitz, the position in the provinces was more problematic. London was too big a target to destroy. The smaller cities experienced less bombing, but the impact was probably greater. MO reckoned that the destruction of the entire city centres of Coventry, Southampton and Portsmouth created the kind of shock that had never really occurred in London. Home Intelligence, once again, was less impressed by the effect on morale, but it could not be denied that the material damage was relatively greater. Coventry, in particular, was hit with unprecedented ferocity and accuracy on 14–15 November, due to the use of navigational radio beams by the Luftwaffe. In a ten-hour attack, one hundred acres of the centre of the city were destroyed, including the Cathedral, for centuries a huge and imposing landmark in such a small, compact city. One-third of the city's houses were destroyed or badly damaged, 554 people killed. MO commented that

> the small size of the place makes people feel that the only thing they can do is get out of it altogether . . . 'Coventry is finished', and 'Coventry is dead' were the key phrases in Friday's talk. . . . There were more open signs of hysteria, terror, neurosis, observed in one evening than during the whole of the past two months together in all areas.[27]

Again, as in the case of the Battle of France, the press did not try to minimize matters. In fact, direct comparisons were made. The *Daily Herald* told the rest of Britain that Coventry resembled a French town levelled by the bombardments of the Great War.

> I approached the city from Rugby, and a few miles out of Coventry I encountered the first large body of refugees walking along the roadside exactly as the Belgians and French escaped from the last German invasion. Children were being carried in their fathers' arms, and pushed along in perambulators. Luggage was piled high in perambulators. There were suitcases and bundles on peoples' shoulders; little families trudged along hand in hand with rugs, blankets and, in fact, anything they could have salved from their ruined homes.

Centre page, the *Herald* could at least claim that the RAF had been 'pounding the great Berlin railway stations and goods yards . . . increasing the transport chaos in Germany'.[28] On the same day, the *Manchester Guardian* led with the story of the RAF raid on Berlin, also claiming that there was worsening chaos in the German transport system. The raid on Coventry was covered in terms of the full Air Ministry communiqué, which admitted that the raid was comparable with the largest attacks on London, that it had caused extensive damage, and the reckoning had reached 1000 casualties. The report continued with the Ministry of Home Security statement that Herbert Morrisson had visited the city, and that he had been 'strongly impressed by the courage and cheerfulness with which the people faced their ordeal'. Below this was the text of a German communiqué which explained that the 'extremely heavy blow' had been delivered as retaliation for a British raid on Munich. On an inside page came a message of sympathy and solidarity from Londoners via the *Guardian*'s London Correspondent.[29]

In the local press, the provincial Blitz was actually used to create civic pride, evidence that provincials could 'take it' just as well as Londoners. Comparisons made in newspapers were often designed to show that the local Blitz had been every bit as bad as the next town's. Portsmouth's *Evening News* on 6 December virtually boasted that Berlin had claimed that the port was the principal target in the previous night's attacks. As was usual in local reports of bombing, the overall story was then individualized: 'South Coast Nurses Brave Night Blitz', 'Bombed Film Fans' Calmness', 'Girl Trapped for 14 Hours: War's Most Heroic Rescue'.[30] There were to be local histories of the Blitz produced in their dozens over the next few years, a large number the work of the local newspapers. Some appeared during the war itself but most were published in the immediate postwar years. Unlike Tom Harrisson's later findings from the MO archive, the large majority of these publications were, as one might expect, uncritical of local reactions. They were often introspective, even parochial in fitting the local story into the national picture.[31] They were constructed both as symbols of local pride and emblems of victory. There was clearly a very large market for these publications, a factor which is itself worth considering. What were people buying? The facts, after all, must have been well known to locals, since they had lived through them. They were surely buying a pattern, a local historical map against which they could orientate their personal and family experience, and thus make sense of their own experience as part of a larger story. Plymouth's record, *It Came to Our Door*, was published in 1945, reprinted three times in 1946, reissued in 1949 and again as late as 1975. Its object was to set everything down for posterity, and the author began by worrying that he might have missed some event, some person, from the record. It listed every raid, every local dignitary, and hailed the rebuilding of the city. Like a memorial, its function is to say 'this happened, and it must not be forgotten'. Buying such a memorial is not like buying a Coronation mug or a poppy; it is a celebration not so much of national survival, but the survival of the local community reflected in the photographs of the streets and people one knows or knew, articulated to a family of cities who all had their battle honours to carry.

The Luftwaffe rarely returned to the same provincial targets the following night, as they did to London. If they had, and if MO were right, the consequences might have been serious. Home Intelligence, working nationally and daily on air-raid morale, emphasized the larger picture, that morale normally fell after a raid, and a number of jittery people might flee, but the large majority of people soon recovered from the shock. People returned to their jobs, cleared up their homes and adapted to the Blitz, not because they were super-patriotic, nor because they were swayed by the propaganda, but because there was no alternative. Life simply had to go on. The M.o.I. was careful to warn the BBC and other commentators neither to generalize on morale nor to overemphasize the need for cheerfulness. After all, why should anybody feel cheerful when their house had been destroyed? The emphasis, the M.o.I. suggested, should be on the future rather than the present.[32]

In some ways, the M.o.I. virtually refused to propagandize during the Blitz. Already rather wary after its experience early on in the war, the M.o.I. had again had its fingers burned by MO criticism of its leaflet on air raids precautions. This pamphlet was apparently not read by a substantial proportion of the population, and not understood by another substantial proportion. One man interviewed had even suggested that the leaflet said that the way to deal with an incendiary bomb was to lie on it.[33] When other ministries asked the M.o.I. how it could publicize services criticized by the public, as often as not the M.o.I. responded that the Ministry should change its services, that there was no point trying to propagandize failure.

> The Government is often accused of being too Olympian. 'White-hall has no contact with the people' is a common accusation. At such a time when the solidarity and resistance – mental, moral and physical – of the whole people is of vital importance . . . it is very wrong if grievances and hardships should be allowed to fester and go unnoticed. We have built up a system whereby we hope to hear all of them; after which we strive to put them right.[34]

Home Intelligence was in the habit of reporting public grumblings, particularly about the failure of post-raid preparations, with evidence that these grumbles were justified. After a raid, it was reported, people needed good information and they needed emergency services. Too often in the early days of the Blitz, these were provided only by the charities, particularly the Women's Voluntary Service (WVS), which did sterling work but was hardly equipped or organized to deal with social disasters of this magnitude. Each provincial city had to relearn on its own, it seemed, the lessons that had been taught by the London Blitz. Home Intelligence was particularly condemnatory in the case of the local authorities in Plymouth and Portsmouth.[35] Far from dreaming up campaigns to maintain morale, the M.o.I. found itself instead in the role of gadfly to the government. As one historian has put it, 'after a period of two or three months from the commencement of intensive bombing . . . there dawned in the Ministry the realization that morale would not break. The British people were sturdy after all. There was no mass panic, no call for peace at any price, no querulous demand for material reward in return for a con-tinued war effort.'[36] But there were grumbles about the failure of the system to feed them when there was no electricity or gas, to rehouse them, and to help them get back to work as soon as possible.

The M.o.I. approved, in other words, of action rather than exhorta-tion, and agreed with the pragmatic, *ad hoc* political changes that occurred in the second half of 1940 in order to cope with the everyday problems of living with the Blitz. The tradition of local independence and self-government was critically undermined by the Blitz and required government intervention. The timely replacement at the Home Office of the prime mover of prewar air raid measures, Sir John Anderson, by Herbert Morrison, former Leader of the London County Council, encouraged a new approach. Morrison took over many of the powers of the local authorities in Stepney and West Ham in November 1940 to try to restore public confidence. One problem was that local Public Assistance Committees (still known as the Poor Law to many working-class people) assumed that most people would and should help themselves.

Rest centres for those made homeless by bombing were designed to provide for up to 10,000 people on any one night, but in London there were 25,000 staying in them by late September. True, these 25,000 were only one-tenth of the number that had been made homeless in total. In a large city like London, friends, relatives and neighbours could indeed soon absorb many of the homeless. This often made, quite literally, for some strange bedfellows, and was the basis of the belief that a 'community spirit' had saved Britain by melting the reserve of the urban population. This still left a very sizeable number of people reliant on the rest centres. Typically, a rest centre was a local school with few blankets and few medical supplies, without even proper toilet facilities. The WVS and the Red Cross did what they could but the Ministry of Health had no option but to intervene, giving the London County Council (LCC) the money and a virtual *carte blanche* to expand and improve them. The Minister of Food, Lord Woolton, also gave the LCC the powers to establish a communal feeding service, which was to include a number of special canteen trains running between the tube stations to feed the shelterers. A Special Regional Commissioner for the Homeless was established by government for the capital. The man appointed was Henry Willink, later wartime Minister of Health and, arguably, a major architect of the National Health Service. By August 1941, over one million houses in London had been made weatherproof.[37]

What had been given to London could hardly be denied the rest of the country when similar problems emerged during the provincial Blitz. By May 1941, post-raid services were working both smoothly and compassionately. As the Blitz ended, in fact, Britain was just about ready for it to start. Once it became clear that the typical air raid victim was not a radical preaching defeatism or class war but a middle-aged man, dressed only in vest and trousers, who had lost his glasses, his false teeth, his ration book and his bicycle, official attitudes changed rapidly. A government that had gone into the war feeling threatened by the possible reactions to bombing of the people who had elected them had, by the end of 1940, in practical terms swilled away the Poor Law mentality. No doubt the impetus for this intervention was practical as much as compassionate, once it became clear that the only threat to morale, and the only real threat to war work, were the detailed difficulties of sorting out one's life in a post-raid city. There was certainly no plan to it; it was *ad hoc*, piecemeal, pragmatic. Nevertheless, something of the old world had died. This was the propaganda of the deed in the Blitz.

The novelist Tom Robbins once wrote appealingly about what he called 'the purple exhaust of myth, through whose plumes events and forces too huge, too complex to easily explain, crystallize into human perspective'.[38] A myth, in the sense that I am using the term, is not necessarily a lie, but rather a story that seeks to explain the larger, impersonal forces of change in terms which make sense to those affected by those changes. It seeks to articulate the different experiences of the many in an overarching and unifying explanation. In the aftermath of a heavy raid, with all their possessions and their homes destroyed, relatives perhaps dead or injured, survivors may well have shown, as Tom Harrisson later described it, 'a hopeless, and indeed helpless incapacity to appreciate the significance of their plight and the reasons for the disaster'.[39] For the survivors, as well as for the majority of the country who were never bombed as well, a truly enormous explanation was required for the unprecedented destruction. Over 40,000 were dead. Nine out of ten houses in Central and Eastern London had been destroyed or damaged, 60 per cent of the houses in Hull. In Clydebank, only seven of the 12,000 houses escaped any damage, and 75 per cent of the population had been made homeless there at some point in the Blitz.

The 'super-truth' the myth of the Blitz offered was that of the moral authority of a people, virtually defenceless against an indiscriminate and brutal attack, responding stoically to the challenge to their community, their families, their civic buildings, their sense of the past and, therefore, their identity in the present. The heroes were not only themselves members of the same communities but also heroes of passive defence, and therefore morally unchallengeable – firemen, air-raid wardens, heavy rescue squads, bomb-disposal squads. The mistakes of the past were put aside as Britain fought on alone at the front line of democracy. St Paul's rode on above the smoke and ruins of a great city, signifying British creative genius as well as her Christian tradition. Coventry Cathedral, conversely and paradoxically, had been levelled by the pagans. The Provost of the Cathedral reflected on radio:

> All through that night the clock ringingly struck the hours and many people far and wide thought the cathedral was all right but there – there it is. That night the city burned and the mother church of the city burned with her. Can't help feeling there's a sort of emblem of the eternal truth that when men suffer, God suffers with them. And yet the tower and the spire still stand, soaring to the sky, and I feel that's an emblem of the eternal majesty and love of God. It was the spirit of our forefathers that built that grand building. I believe that the spirit is with us still and will help us to rebuild it when we've served and suffered a while, a little longer – build it again to the glory of Jesus Christ.[40]

The tower still stood; the rest would be rebuilt, as Britain herself would arise, phoenix-like, from her own ashes. For the moment, reconstruction was only a dream for the future, but the scale of destruction made it an inescapable problem for the political class, and an unprecedented opportunity for the professionals of the civic services to make their plans. The Blitz also made it that much easier to contemplate visiting the same fate on the enemy. While the cities of Germany were to suffer much worse in the next few years, it would be difficult to make the British believe that their bombing had not been the first and therefore the more heroic, and the more spiritual, stand. Eventual victory 'proved' that Britain could take it and Germany could not. The Blitz justified too a sense of apocalyptic vengeance. As 'Bomber' Harris had commented quietly as he watched the Blitz from an Air Ministry building – with characteristic downbeat malevolence – 'well, they are sewing the wind.'[41]

6 Wartime politics and popular culture

The coalition that came into being on 10 May 1940 might easily have been undone within months, had it not been for the events, which succeeded it – the defeat in France, the threat of invasion, the Battle of Britain, the Blitz. Right-wing, patrician political figures such as Winston Churchill had virtually nothing in common with working-class champions such as Ernest Bevin, except a shared belief that Chamberlain's appeasement had left Britain perilously exposed. If, as might easily have happened, the tide in France had been stemmed and the Western Front had settled into a technologically updated version of 1914–1918, one can imagine political infighting developing along even more ferocious lines than those of the Great War. Churchill was mistrusted by many Conservatives, as well as the Opposition, as being a turncoat, an extremist, as a politician more fond of rhetoric and dreams than practicalities. Few would have shared the new Prime Minister's confidence as he walked with destiny in May. As it was, in the early months of the new government as Churchill sought to establish his position, there were only two Labour ministers in a War Cabinet which in effect continued to be dominated by the two most experienced members, Neville Chamberlain and Lord Halifax. Not until Chamberlain's illness and retirement in October was Churchill able to secure his own position by becoming Leader of the Conservative Party. Halifax was then levered out of the Cabinet and into the Washington Embassy in December.

Even then, prominent prewar politicians who were at least tainted with the 'Guilty Men' malaise remained in significant positions – Kingsley Wood as Chancellor of the Exchequer until his death in 1942, and Sir John Anderson as Home Secretary until October 1940 and, later, successor to Wood at the Exchequer. In a War Cabinet that varied between eleven and fourteen members over the war, there were only five Labour men. In the twenty-odd Cabinet ministries outside the War Cabinet, only six Labour men achieved office, and two of those were among the five already noted as sometime members of the War Cabinet.

The new government is said to have represented the wish of the people. It would be churlish to point out that the people had not actually spoken in 1940. The Churchill coalition was the result of a revolution in the Palace of Westminster, in which Labour had refused to serve with Chamberlain, not a general election. The last two general elections had in fact been resounding victories for MacDonald, Baldwin and Chamberlain, and the next was actually to see the resounding defeat of Churchill. But the circumstances of the second half of 1940 meant that, in effect, willy-nilly, Churchill was Britain's destiny. Though there were to be a few occasions during the war when he came under pressure, his position was to be virtually unassailable by the end of 1940. His popularity rating was regularly above 80 per cent, much higher than that of the government as a whole.[1]

The Guilty Men thesis cast the blame for defeat in 1940 on a cowardly lack of leadership in the interwar years, reversed by the historic partnership of Churchill and Labour at the forefront of a 'people's war'. Such a notion of the wartime coalition as a signifier of a wider unity in British society was strengthened by particular readings of the different practical crises through which Britain passed in 1940, covered in the last three chapters. The purpose of this chapter and those that follow is to show how these myths of a united, heroic, decent, progressive, put-upon nation developed as the immediate crises fell into the past, and how the myth shifted its meaning and implications through later crises.

On the one hand, for the mainstream Left, the political implication of these myths was that 1940 was the moment when Labour came into its legacy, when the working class showed its true muscle in resisting the bombs and in developing the tools for victory over fascism, led by Labour ministers who showed that they had the organizational skills and other powers of leadership necessary to lead the people. Labour thus gave the lie to the taunt of the 1920s and 1930s that it was unfit to govern. Labour membership of the government may not have been strong numerically, but Herbert Morrison as Home Secretary and Ernest Bevin as Minister of Labour impinged on the daily lives of people on the home front even more than Churchill. The Prime Minister was a grand and military figure, not an everyday maker of practical policy in terms of production quotas, labour regulation, wages, post-raid and other welfare services.

Seen from this perspective, 1945 was simply a resounding vote of confidence in the men who had led Britain on the home front for the previous five years. By the late 1960s, however, with the apparent failure of democratic socialism to make any real impact on entrenched capitalism, the New Left was to reject the triumphs of Labour's 'High Noon' as mere compromise. From the perspective of the right, on the other hand, 1940 was the moment when Labour's collectivism usurped the rightful position of Conservatism. Churchill, for all his significance as a national leader and figurehead, failed to give a lead to his party at home. In so doing, he was politically inept enough to allow Labour to lead a drift to the Left in wartime, which culminated in their victory at the polls in 1945, hijacking the victory for freedom for which Britain had fought so hard and so long and, for a crucial year and a half, alone. Although the Conservatives were to be in power from 1951 to 1964, and to modify Labour's collectivism in the name of Tory reform, for the New Right this was simply playing Labour at its own game. As a result, the New Right had to wait until the late 1970s before it could begin to roll back the state-interventionist tide.

These interpretations stem from different readings of the events of 1940. The readings often overlap, but they work within different frameworks. The first interpretation stresses the significance of the national family. It highlights notions of community and of rescue in the little boats at Dunkirk, in the factory workers who worked day and night to produce the Spitfires, in the plight of the evacuees, in the role of the community heroes of the Blitz. It stresses Priestley's gentle homilies. It stresses defence rather than offence. Though Lucy Noakes would not entirely accept my reading in her book on gender and national identity, it still seems to me that this construction of the war highlights, at its most basic, 'feminized' values – introspective, caring and sharing – which transformed the warfare state into the welfare state.[2] The other is more obviously masculist, stressing male heroism in terms of national defiance rather than mere defence and protection, in the case of the little boats as well as the firemen of the Blitz, the significance of 'the few' in the Battle of Britain, the bulldog spirit of Churchill and his flowing, nationalist rhetoric, focusing Britain as the champion of liberty while the other democracies failed or dithered.

Churchill's own history of the war was to be enormously influential in the immediately succeeding years. Lionized wherever he went as the man who had foreseen the danger of Hitler, who had been left in the political wilderness as a result, who had then been summoned to save England in her hour of peril, and had gone from near absolute defeat to eventual victory, his writings on the war took on the status of sacred text. Churchill's postwar writing on the war took up seamlessly from and filled the gaps left by his exhilarating wartime speeches. No one on the Left could carry and focus the British crusade as personally and as charismatically as Churchill could for the Right; and Churchill's was, of course, a very personal history of the war. He could claim to have been there, at the very centre of things, at a time when Roosevelt was dead and Stalin was not forthcoming. He did not claim it to be history in itself but he did claim it as a contribution to history, when that history eventually came to be written. Understandably, his story of the war is very Anglocentric. There is rather more on the European than on the Pacific war, except where it directly relates to the British Empire. While giving full weight to the enormous impact of the Americans on the outcome of the war – 'our greatest Ally' – he is keen to point out that more British than Americans were killed, and that until the last year of the war there were more British in direct contact with enemy armed forces than Americans. 'This is all set down, not to claim undue credit, but to establish on a footing capable of commanding fair-minded respect the intense output in every form of war activity of the people of this small Island, upon whom in the crisis of the world's history the brunt fell'.[3]

About the Soviet Union, he was rather more sanguine. While admitting that the Soviets were to break the back of the German armed forces, he was at pains to point out that for at least the first year of the German–Soviet conflict, the Soviet Union was more of a burden to the allies than a help. But at this remove in time, what emerges from the work is the extraordinary spirit of magnanimity in which it is written, a spirit of generosity towards virtually everybody except, of course, the Axis leadership. Even Stalin's eyes could 'twinkle with mirth and good humour'. It is, of course, a magnanimity that comes only with victory, with having been proved absolutely right after long-term vilification.

British politics in the war do not figure significantly in Churchill's memoir, except in 1939 and 1940, the year of his own rise to pre-eminence. Chamberlain, for all his faults in the 1930s, emerges as a brave man who took his replacement by Churchill in a dignified and loyal manner and, even in his final illness, 'kept all his appointments, and he was never more spick and span or cool than at the last cabinets which he attended'. When it was clear that Chamberlain was too ill to continue after his operation, Churchill suggests that he virtually had to order him to go away to get well: 'I never saw him again. I am sure he wanted to die in harness. This was not to be.'[4] Churchill's Chamberlain is a tragic figure, not the gullible fool of Guilty Men: 'unhappily he ran into tides the force of which he could not measure, and met hurricanes from which he did not flinch, but with which he could not cope.'[5] Neither Labour nor Liberals were in a position to throw stones, given their equal failure in the 1930s to measure the threat of Hitler, as shown by their long opposition to rearmament. Churchill accepted that many Conservatives were resentful of him, that they cheered Chamberlain in the House of Commons rather than him, but he suggested that he resisted a campaign to purge the Guilty Men not for political reasons, but because patriotic, experienced and able men continued to be needed in the crisis: 'No one had more right than I to pass a sponge across the past.'[6] Unfortunately for Churchill's political future, his personal lack of responsibility for the 'locust years', and his personal magnanimity to the Guilty Men, was not to shield the rest of his party. The War Cabinet gradually left more and more of the military and strategic aspects of the war to Churchill, as both Prime Minister and Minister of Defence. In a telling sentence, which suggests another reason why he lost the 1945 General Election, he mentions that 'They took almost the whole weight of home and party affairs off my shoulders, thus setting me free to concentrate upon the main theme.'[7]

The main theme, of course, was the military, the eventually heroic one as far as Churchill was concerned. What of 'the people' in all this? They feature rather nebulously in his story. Churchill assumes that he was able to express the sentiments of 'almost all the people' in the crisis of 1940, because their sentiments were also his. He describes his role as an articulation of the transcendent spirit of the nation in 1940. 'There was a white glow, overpowering, sublime which ran through our Island from end to end'. It was this which prompted the 'spontaneous movement which swept the sea-faring population of our southern and south-eastern shores' at the time of Dunkirk. Yet his meetings with these people are sporadic, distanced. In passing, he tells of being on a visit to Ramsgate when an air raid occurred, 'and I was conducted into their big tunnel, where quite large numbers of people lived permanently'. The result was his 'immediate resolve' that all damage to housing must become a charge on the state, which resulted in persuading the Chancellor to accept the insurance scheme which was devised over the next fortnight.[8]

There are chirpy cockney sparrows, such as the concierge at the club in St James who welcomed downcast members after the Battle of France with the observation that 'at least it means we're in the final, and playing at home'. But his real heroes on the home front are those who stood out from the crowd, the unexploded bomb (UXB) detachments, volunteers for the game of Russian roulette with a delayed-action fuse. 'Somehow or other their faces seemed different from those of ordinary men, however brave and faithful. They were gaunt, haggard, their faces had a bluish look, with bright gleaming eyes and exceptional compression of the lips.' Even then, in his patrician way, it is a UXB team led by the Earl of Suffolk which he singles out for mention, killed while working on their thirty-fifth bomb. 'Very quickly, but at heavy sacrifice of our noblest, the devotion of the UXB detachments mastered the peril.'[9]

It is on the few rather than the many that Churchill's focus rests. The many are a homogenized mass, 'the nation', though certainly the 'nation was as sound as the sea is salt'. '"London could take it". They took all they got, and could have taken more.' For all the admitted suffering of the urban populations of Britain, for Churchill the 'climax raid' of the Blitz was the fire raid on the City of London on 29 December, a raid which destroyed far fewer buildings and resulted in fewer deaths than many other raids, but in which so much of British heritage was targeted and destroyed: 'Eight (*sic*) Wren churches were destroyed or damaged. The Guildhall was smitten by fire and blast, and St Paul's Cathedral was only saved by heroic exertions. A void of ruin at the very centre of the British world gaped upon us.'[10]

While Churchill's version of 1940 rested on a glorious view of English culture and the English past, and the assumption that the true English destiny had yet to be fulfilled (eliding, of course, Englishness with Britishness in the traditional hegemonic way), the liberal Left intelligentsia projected recent events as both progenitor and signifier of the massive changes that the war would bring about. For Churchill, 1940 was about continuity, for the liberal Left it was about a necessary though quiet revolution. In George Orwell, the writer who came closer than any other to finding the left-wing shorthand for the war that Churchill invented for the Right, it was the subtle blend of patriotism and millenarianism that was to prove so powerfully seductive as a credo for British social democracy. Orwellism depended on no foreign creed; his experience in Spain had taught him that the Marxists were as bad as the Fascists. He wrote that he dreamed in late August 1939 that the war had already started, that when he woke up he heard that the Nazi–Soviet Pact had been signed and that war was now indeed inevitable – and that once England was in a serious jam it would be impossible for me to sabotage. But let no one mistake the meaning of this. Patriotism has nothing to do with conservatism. It is devotion to something that is changing but is felt to the mystically the same. . . . Only revolution can save England, that has been obvious for years, but now the revolution has started, and it may proceed quite quickly if only we can keep Hitler out. . . . But when the red militias are billeted in the Ritz I shall still feel that the England I was taught to love so long ago and for such different reasons is somehow persisting.[11]

By the time of 'The lion and the unicorn', Orwell was even less scared of revolutionism, because he believed it would be undertaken in a quiet, more 'English' way. The most famous construction of this essay, that England was a family with the wrong members in control, was an appropriation of the English family ideology from the upper classes and from the political Right, articulating it instead to a gentle left-wing tradition. The war, he felt, confirmed this shift in the dominant class identity of Britain. Foreigners who had come to England during the war as soldiers or as refugees, 'to whom England meant Piccadilly and the Derby found themselves quartered in sleepy East Anglian villages, in northern mining towns, or in the vast working-class areas of London whose names the world had never heard until they were blitzed'.[12] Gradually, as they were targeted, and as they were called upon to save England, the real English people were waking up to their powers as well as their responsibilities.

Of course, George Orwell never had the kind of mass audience that Churchill enjoyed as Prime Minister in wartime, or as public hero after the war. In a smaller way, however, the war significantly changed his ability to be heard. Not only did he become a patriot of sorts, which made him politically more acceptable (like the authors of *Guilty Men*), but his period as literary editor of the *Tribune* brought him close to some leading left-wing figures, Aneurin Bevan in particular, and earned him a readership among the left-wing intelligentsia more generally. His new-found confidence that he was speaking from the inside rather than the outside was reflected in similar ways by Left-liberals working at the BBC, in the cinema, and in the press. While Churchill's voice may have been both massive and irrefutable on the larger scale, there was a daily drip-drip of left-liberalism in mass communications to which there were very few right-wing replies. Orwell commented that to find any expression of right-wing opinion by the mid-war period, one had to go to obscure, largely Catholic weeklies and monthlies.[13] The kind of sentiments that had already been expressed in *Times* leaders during the Blitz were given sharper form and focus by the 'Plan for Britain' published by *Picture Post* in the first few days of 1941. It was not, *Picture Post* declared, simply a plan for the distant future, but a necessity for the here and now.

> It is an essential part of our war aims. It is, indeed, our most positive war aim. The new Britain is the country we are fighting for. And the kind of land we want, the kind of life we think the good life, will exercise an immense attraction over the oppressed peoples of Europe and the friendly peoples of America.[14]

Not only was it important that the British, their allies and their enemies knew what the British were fighting for – which was not, it was implied, the greater glory of Britain but the furtherance of social democracy – but the first year of the war had shown what needed to be done and how it could be done. The demand was there, but so also was the opportunity and the methodology. Above all – and this was central not just to *Picture Post*'s argument but to the whole discourse on reconstruction as it developed – there was an assumption that such change would move forward consensually, as a matter of common sense:

> The war has been not only a personal crisis for each one of us. It has been a crisis for our country's whole economic and political life. We have been forced into a knowledge of our dependence on each other. . . . We believe that, after this war, certain things will be common ground among all political parties. It will be common ground, for example, that every Briton – man, woman or child – shall be assured of enough food of the right kinds to maintain him in full bodily health and fitness. It will be common ground that we must reform our system of education – so that every child is assured of the fullest education he can profit by. It will be common ground that our state medical service must be reorganized and developed so as to foster health, not merely battle with disease. It will be common ground that the agricultural land of Britain must not be given up to thistles and bracken; and that the beauty of our country and our buildings is the nation's heritage, not to be pawned away in plots to speculative builders.[15]

What followed is one of the most obvious examples of the new confidence in 'expertism', a sense that the professional and his scientific rationalism should be put at the service of humanity, in place of the haphazard amateurism that had contributed so significantly to the present disaster.

First, an 'ordinary' working-class man was called upon to state the problem. An unemployed miner, formerly an unemployed agricultural worker (thus combining the two heroic traditions of the working class) complained about the waste of unemployment when so much was needed from these great industries in such a war. Looking back on the great mistakes of Spain and Czechoslovakia in the 1930s, he calculated that

> Those blunders have finished for ever the tradition of a class that was born to govern; and educated to believe that only the best was good enough for them . . . I feel there must be great changes in the men and women who run this country. There must be new ideas and new methods.[16]

In fact, this spokesperson for the working class was no 'ordinary man' at all; it was B.L. Coombes, the articulate and passionate author of *These Poor Hands*, soon to be established as one of the most significant proletarian novels of the 1930s.[17] Following Coombes came a stream of 'acknowledged experts in their field', including Thomas Balogh on full employment, A.D.K. Owen on social security, Maxwell Fry on town planning, A.D. Lindsay on education, Julian Huxley on health. The emphasis throughout was on planning, on controls, on scrapping old attitudes, on using the experience of the war so far to understand that a nation could do virtually what it wanted when it wanted, as long as it was planned. None of this, the experts suggested, was pie in the sky. It was, rather, a practical application of the results of investigations made in so many areas in the prewar years married to the interventionist politics that 1940 had made necessary to survive the war.

Profusely illustrated, as always, this issue reused many of *Picture Post*'s iconographic photographs of the depression years, contrasting them with the brave new world of bright factories, 'spacious' workers' housing, the scale model for the reconstruction of Coventry – indeed, virtually all those tokens of postwar Britain that a new generation was demanding should be pulled down in the 1970s. There was none of the impassioned revolutionism of the Left Book Club, nor even accusations of negligence à la Guilty Men. Instead, there was the application of pragmatism, on the basis of statistics, investigation and scientific rationalism. These were not dreams, the authors implied, but simple, practical and necessary politics.

Such interventions should come to be considered the norm, in a normal society. But, again as a matter of fact, things were not normal at the time. In relation to town planning:

> As I write, bombs are dropping on London and fire is raging. Some people imagine that what is destroyed is a good riddance. This is mistaken, because bombing is haphazard, and the bad street plan, which bombs never really destroy, is the root evil. But when people say, as they do, that the East End of London is no loss to us, they make a confession of real relief that they have no longer to answer their consciences for those slums and muddles. They hope to rebuild to better standards. They begin, in fact, to have a real 'will' to plan.[18]

It is not quite clear as to the identity of these people who were suggesting that the East End was no loss. Presumably, it was not East Enders themselves, and probably not the majority of readers of *Picture Post*. While Churchill provided a vision of including the vast majority of British people in a hitherto somewhat alien empire as it passed through its 'finest hour', the experts of welfarism told the same British people that the alternative vision of the 1930s intelligentsia was now theirs for the asking. These were invitations to live in two different but equally unfamiliar worlds, as far as the large majority in Britain were concerned.

These were not alternative workings of 1940 at the time, of course, because they could co-exist. Why should the inhabitants of the largest empire there had ever been not live in what they were told was decent housing, and enjoy full employment and a decent health service? Many of the liberal left intelligentsia could have subscribed to the view that the empire should be transformed into a co-operative Commonwealth rather than be simply disbanded, and would be closer to Churchill than to, say, the Americans on imperialism. What was on offer was a picture of Britain supreme in the world but enjoying the standard of living that was accepted through America and much of Europe, including British enemies in Germany. What would be the point of fighting for anything less? For the time being the liberal left critiques of the 1930s did not actually connect with the fact of empire: they were two different worlds. Britain was isolationist by force of circumstances in 1940, and the first explanations that had to be given were domestic rather than international. How had things gone so awry? How could the situation be rectified?

In 1941, and in the ensuing war years, the gulf between the 1930s and the present, opened by *Guilty Men* – by Muggeridge and by Graves and Hodge in 1940 – was widened, reinforced, entrenched. An early example was the film of Walter Greenwood's *Love on the Dole*. Three attempts to film the novel in the 1930s had run up against censorship problems. Finally filmed in 1940 and released in 1941, it sailed through the censors, probably because it placed the Depression firmly in the distant past, and as a counterpoint to the present. The opening rolling caption read:

> This film recalls one of the darker pages of our industrial history. On the outskirts of every city, there is a region of darkness and poverty where men and women strive for ever to live decently in face of overwhelming odds, never doubting that the clouds of depression will one day be lifted. Such a district was Hanky Part in March 1930.[19]

March 1930 was only just over a decade past in 1941, but some of the costumes used in the film suggest a period somewhat further in the past – the early 1920s at least, if not the Edwardian period. Greenwood's novel was about people who could see no hope, no way out of the Depression and its impact on everything down to personal morality. The film, on the other hand, was about people waiting for a moment which would certainly come. That moment, it is clear in the film, is the war, the moment when 'we'll all be wanted again'. The strategic assumption made in such material is that everybody already knew that those were the bad times and those bad times are over, whereas that assumption was actually being constructed in such material. At the end of *Love on the Dole*, another rolling caption quoted the words of A.V. Alexander, a Labour member of the government:

> Our working men and women have responded magnificently to any and every call made upon them in this war. Their reward must be a New Britain. Never again must the unemployed become the forgotten men of the peace.

Greenwood's originally dark, gloomy, pessimistic account of life on the dole was thus transformed into the clarion call of a people's war, re-focusing representations of the 1930s in the process.

The documentary film-makers, on the periphery of cinema in the 1930s, were taken over lock, stock and barrel by the M.o.I. as the Crown Film Unit in 1940. Understandably, they took their politics with them, a somewhat anodyne liberal-socialism. Their material, going out from 1940 under the imprint of the M.o.I. and bearing the image of the Crown to show that it was official information, rarely missed an opportunity to picture the war as a radical struggle to make sure that the 1930s never happened again. Dylan Thomas intoned on the soundtrack of one such film, *Wales, Green Mountain, Black Mountain*, over footage of unemployed men in the Welsh valleys in the 1930s:

> Remember the procession of the old young men.
> From dole queue to corner and back again
> Nothing in their pockets
> Nothing home to eat
> Nothing but the corner of the cold, pinched street
> It must never happen again
> It shall never happen again.[20]

One of the central strategies of wartime representations of the interwar period was to borrow the armoury of war memorialization, the modes of address normally associated with Armistice Day. In the soundtrack, spoken as well as written by Thomas at this point, the injunction 'Remember' is highly emphatic. This is spoken over pictures of slow-moving unemployed men. 'Never again' was a stock phrase in newsreel and newspaper coverage of Armistice Day in the interwar period. When taken with the contemporary demonization of the interwar political leaders, the unemployed of the 1930s become the new lions led by donkeys. It is an act both of commemoration and communion which is structured here, which also necessarily involves a commitment to the future. By 1945, Humphrey Jennings could come up with the most astonishing interconnections between the interwar and the war years. In his film *Diary for Timothy* in 1945, charting the first days of life of baby Timothy as the war in Europe comes to its conclusion, he could picture Timothy safe and warm in his pram but warn that 'it wouldn't be like this if you had been born in war-torn Czecho-slovakia or Poland, or a Glasgow or Liverpool slum'. There is not even a hint of worry that the connection between the experience of occupied Europe and the depressed areas of Britain in the 1930s would be scoffed at.[21] So far had 'common sense' travelled in the war.

Whatever government wanted or hoped, such projections of what made the 1930s different from the 1940s appear to have passed without question. The pragmatic reaction of government in 1940, based on the need to offset relatively minor but still complicated problems of post-raid welfare and to get people back to essential war work, created a situation in which the traditional ideology of non-interventionist government visibly cracked. The piecemeal evolution of welfarist ideas, slowly developing as they had since the turn of the twentieth century, took a major leap forward in such circumstances. It simply could not be maintained, as in some circles it still could be in the Depression, that the working class had only themselves to blame if they did not take care of themselves and respond to change. Workers were in trouble because they were targets, and they were targets because their contribution to the war effort was vital. In addition, for the first time, middle-class claimants found themselves in the social service queues, doing much to dispel the stigma that had been applied to welfare for over a century. By the end of 1940, the Treasury was paying out to local authorities virtually whatever they said they needed to cope with post-raid problems. This would have been unthinkable even three years previously, but the priority was now national survival, not saving the economy.

In many areas of public life, emergency political omelettes had been hastily cooked which proved impossible to unscramble later. The hospital service was one significant example. In a bid to deal with the mass of casualties, especially psychiatric casualties, expected to result from bombing, the government had financed a regional grouping of hospitals in the Emergency Hospital Service. In fact, there were never less than 20,000 unoccupied hospital beds during the Blitz at a time when there were 20,000 homeless who were not catered for.[22] Because of the expected size of the emergency, nobody had thought much about how the old system would be reintroduced after the war. The problems that would beset the voluntary hospitals made it clear that a return to the old system would be virtually impossible. So the government was to agree to a National Hospital Service, a virtual nationalization of the system, which in turn made it that much easier to contemplate a National Health Service as the next pragmatic and logical step. This development, it should be emphasized, was the result of something not happening, or, at least, not happening on the scale that had been expected. Again, given the scale of the emergency, Keynes was appointed to a post in the Treasury to advise on policy in a period of massive overspending.[23] Beveridge began work in a similarly pragmatic atmosphere, in which prewar expectations had proved wrong and solutions had to be found quickly, rather than economically.

In practice, the emergency had created in Whitehall a climate in which virtually every principle of government was up for grabs, a climate in which the architects of the Welfare State could move much more easily. In turn, these *ad hoc* and largely piecemeal, short-term shifts in governmental attitudes towards the problems of dealing with total war were given shape and direction, were made to make sense in terms, first, of a rejection of the Guilty Men and all that they were now deemed to have stood for, and, second, an assumption that everybody would be prepared to accept such change consensually. The government had not even considered its attitude towards social reconstruction as yet, but in a sense it was too late. It was already happening, as the nation helped return the men from Dunkirk, as the factories blasted out maximum production, as the fighter pilots fought above England's green and pleasant land, as the Blitz added the imagery of fire and redemption. A series of short-term governmental changes to deal with an emergency, which had been wrongly perceived, was patterned into an apparently radical and irreversible change in the nature of the relationship between nation and state. The nation had saved the state and now the state would grow with the people.

In the realm of high politics, Kevin Jefferys has argued convincingly that there never really was a consensus on reconstruction. In answer to Paul Addison's argument that during the war there occurred a switch in politics from Baldwin's consensus to Attlee's consensus, Jefferys argued that in fact the wartime government could agree on very little except the need not to argue publicly in view of the crisis. Churchill was not interested in the Beveridge Report, if only because he felt it promised more for the indefinite future than any one government could guarantee. Most of the White-paper chase that followed Beveridge wallowed in a mire. The National Health Service may have been agreed at the level of principle, but there were major differences of opinion about implementation. A commitment to full employment after the war was hedged around with all sorts of caveats about the probable state of the national finances as the nation re-entered peacetime practice. Only the 1944 Education Act, a somewhat anodyne and long overdue piece of legislation, got on to the statute books before 1945, along with wholly uncontentious measures covering family allowances, free milk and orange juice for children. When the Labour NEC forced a reluctant Labour leadership to pledge large-scale nationalization, the coalition simply and quickly fell apart. Far from being a united front, the coalition could not even fight one general election as a unity, and could not even wait for the end of the war against Japan to force the issue.[24]

The Beveridge Report itself, most historians would now probably agree, was no revolutionary document. It was suffused with the spirit of liberal individualism in its reliance on the contributory system and in its reluctance to undercut the free market principle in relation to wages. It codified and extended existing practice in the social services; in many ways it was a bureaucrat's way of tidying up a messy system.[25] Yet it is still important to emphasize the significance of Beveridge's organizing principles of universality and comprehensiveness, his assumption that, if implemented, his report should guarantee a system of social safety nets for virtually any misfortune that might occur to anyone 'from cradle to grave', and that everybody in the nation should be equally responsible financially, however invulnerable. Though it may have been traditionalist in many of its details, the Beveridge Report was often enlivened with a rhetoric which suggested that it offered more: 'a revolutionary moment in the world's history is a time for revolutions, not for patching', Beveridge declared, though later in the document he claimed that the main thrust was evolutionary, which made it specifically a 'British revolution'. But his most successful projection of the problem was that of the five giants that stood on the road to reconstruction: want, disease, ignorance, squalor and idleness. Here was an apocalyptic vision to appeal to a nation that had got used to apocalyptic images in 1940.

Since I am concerned here not so much with the substance of wartime politics as with their appearance, it should be pointed out that Beveridge clearly came to mean something significant to the public, however much many of those in government tried to shelve it. The Report was especially important in its timing, being published between news of the British victory at the Battle of El Alamein and news of the Russian victory at Stalingrad. Britain had survived 1940, but since then she had been catastrophically defeated in the Far East and suffered grievous shortages as a result of the Battle of the Atlantic. Suddenly, a beam of sunlight began to shine from the end of the long tunnel into the future. Britain was not going to lose; in fact she was going to win; not just yet, but eventually. It was possible, finally, to begin to think realistically about a postwar world, and the Report gave first concrete shape to all the vaguely formulated projections of a fairer society that had laced *Times* and *Guardian* editorials, *Picture Post*, Priestley broadcasts and M.o.I. films since 1940.

Copies of the Report, and a much shorter summary, sold about 650,000 copies in the ensuing months, wholly unprecedented for an official government paper. The BBC World Service began publishing details of the Report in over twenty languages, as an ideological counter-offensive aimed both at the Nazi New Order and the communists, and also, no doubt, to appeal to New Deal sympathies in the United States. RAF bombers dropped pamphlets over Germany explaining the proposals. A Gallup Poll, two weeks after the publication, revealed that 95 per cent of the population had heard the details of the Report, and that 90 per cent wanted the proposals adopted.[26] The *Daily Mirror* warned that Beveridge represented only the first steps towards what was really required in reconstruction, and the *New Statesman* was clearly worried that the most important comprehensive and universal principles in Beveridge should not be whittled down by a lukewarm government.[27] The large majority of the press accepted the Report enthusiastically. Really for the first and only time, the right-wing press tried to make some sort of a stand. The *Daily Telegraph* damned the Report with faint praise as a plan for a 'safety first' society, and commented that the British individualist tradition would never have spread itself so effectively over the whole globe if such a scheme had been in force in the past.[28]

The government faced its biggest backbench revolt of the war over the Report. After the Cabinet agreed to accept the majority of the Report, but only in principle, almost the entire backbench Labour Party voted against the government, even with an intervention from Herbert Morrison. By the end of the year, the Tory Reform Committee had emerged as a ginger group on the Tory Left, urging a much more positive attitude towards social reform. Churchill, however, was largely contemptuous of Beveridge. Though a Reconstruction Priorities Committee was set up, it proved unwieldy in reaching decisions. While Labour members of the War Cabinet fought for detailed plans and financial forecasts to help implement them, they were constantly frustrated by Churchill's lack of interest and the Chancellor's grumblings about the huge costs. *The Economist* voiced the frustrations of the would-be planners:

> ground word is laid upon ground work. But the questions that matter most to the people of this country, the questions of highest policy – the prevention of want, the use and control of the land, the realities of demobilization, industrial re-equipment – all these must apparently remain without even interim replies, and certainly without legislative answers, so long as the voice of Downing Street cannot find time from its vast strategic exercises to speak or to choose a spokesman in its stead.[29]

According to Jefferys, it was only under sustained pressure that Churchill agreed to the setting up of a Ministry of Reconstruction in November 1943. The appointment of the conservative Lord Woolton as the new Minister assured that Labour would not have its head in reconstruction, and since the powers of the Ministry were limited to the co-ordination of plans emerging from other ministries, it could provide no effective lead. As a result, by the end of the war, a number of White Papers had emerged, but most of them were hesitant on the most contentious and significant of issues. The Education Act of 1944 was the only major element in the Beveridge proposals to reach the statute books before the end of the war – largely, Jefferys suggests, because it caused so little dissension, was long overdue, and cost relatively little.[30]

While the rejection in 1940 of the political values of the 1930s was given firm shape by the Beveridge Report, the party political truce disguised the swing to the Left that was happening in the country, fuelled by the revolution in rising expectations engineered by the media. While Labour could not technically challenge coalition partners in by-elections in wartime, the 1941 Committee and then the Common Wealth Party were certainly able to do so, with some spectacular results, many of them clearly with at least tacit local backing from Labour. Even the Communist Party won a very respectable 15 per cent of the vote in the Dunbarton by-election in 1941.

Increasingly, local Labour parties were prepared to break the party truce in order to back Independents in Tory seats. In June 1942, Tom Driberg won Maldon on a 1941 Committee ticket but, clearly, with the backing of local Labour. In 1942 and beyond, the electorate appeared to have serious concerns that the Conservative Party had no real commitment to reject the social values of the Guilty Men after all. Having worked together successfully to meet the crisis of 1940, local councils were increasingly to be divided along the old political lines by the Coalition's failure to give firm leadership to a completion of the revolution in government's role that had been implied by the emergency. Priestley's warning, in his last *Postscript* of 1940, that as the high mood of the crisis passed, greed and self-interest might return, appeared acutely focused.

It is symptomatic of the fact that the reforming spirit of 1940 was at its strongest among the professional middle class that new radical political groupings such as Common Wealth were based largely on support from this group. MO suggested that traditional Labour voters were rather more cynical about what could be achieved, but Labour clearly benefited indirectly from the mauling that Common Wealth gave the Conservatives in three by-elections. Fighting on the slogans 'Common Ownership', 'Vital Democracy' and 'Morality in Politics', Common Wealth chose young heroes to fight their cause – for instance, a Battle of Britain pilot at Eddisbury, and a young army officer at

Skipton. By early 1944, however, Labour began to steal Common Wealth's thunder, particularly when the Labour candidate in West Derbyshire resigned from the party to stand against the Cavendish family of the Dukes of Devonshire, who had represented the constituency for generations. A Tory majority of 5000 was turned into an independent socialist majority of 4500. When the Labour conference refused to affiliate Common Wealth later in the year, Common Wealth was left with no opportunity to leap-frog into the political big time. Labour had ensured that the radical groundswell would fall in with the mainstream Left in a future general election. Still, as the end of the war loomed, most political pundits could not imagine that Churchill, the national saviour in the summer of 1940, could possibly lose.

The 1945 General Election was to prove a bitter contest, underlining just how much the apparent unity imposed on Britain by the crisis of 1940 was subject to very different interpretations and understandings. No doubt the Labour leadership would have preferred to continue the Coalition, assuming as did most others that Churchill would walk the contest. But the Labour NEC was adamant that Labour must be allowed to campaign for nationalization, and the Coalition collapsed as quickly as it had been formed. Churchill's caretaker Cabinet offered little to the Tory Left, suggesting instead a return to traditionalist Conservatism. The campaign was dominated in its early stages by Churchill's extraordinarily tasteless claim that his former colleagues would need 'some form of Gestapo' to introduce their reforms. Former brothers-in-arms in the post-Dunkirk production drive, Beaverbrook and Bevin, were daggers drawn over labour controls. The successful wartime Minister of Information, Brendan Bracken, fought and lost a truculent campaign in North Paddington, where his scaremongering over socialist economic policy provoked a fire-bomb at his headquarters and stones through his car windows.

Although, on the face of it, Churchill's Four Year Plan covered the same sort of ground as Labour's carefully worked out proposals, there were actually major differences in approach with essentially different implications for the future of Britain. The Conservatives maintained that the commitment to full employment was dependent on a sound and flourishing economy, without committing themselves to Keynesian demand management. Tory views on a National Health Service included a commitment to maintain the voluntary hospitals and private practice. In the case of housing and town planning, the single most important election issue after the destruction of 1940 and 1941, Conservatives remained vague while Labour committed itself to long-term planning of the whole of the British physical environment, urban and rural.

In short, the Conservatives fought for a rapid reversal of the kind of controls that the emergency of 1940 had made necessary, a return to freedom; that, after all, was what the war had been fought for: 'Britain's greatness has been built on character and daring, not on docility to a State machine. At all costs we must preserve that spirit of independence and that "right to live by no man's leave underneath the law".'[31] Labour fought not only for the retention of such controls but for their further development into a fully comprehensive social plan to be overseen by demand management; that, rather, was what the war had been fought for. Set firmly in the perspective provided by *Guilty Men*, Labour's manifesto claimed that the people 'deserve and must be assured a happier future than faced so many after the last war.'[32] The Conservative manifesto pictured 1940 as the beginning of a great opportunity, which would continue after the war had been won, for Britain to save the world from tyranny and to play her part in its wise guidance. Labour claimed that no single leader or even set of men could claim credit for victory: the war had been won by the people, and Labour had spoken for the people on 'that fateful day in May, 1940', when the party had brought about the fall of Chamberlain and helped form the new government which had led the country to victory. In such ways were the variant myths of 1940 ranged against each other in 1945. For the moment, the collectivist myth had won the day.

Stunning though the victory for the Labour Party was in 1945, Churchill might have taken some comfort from the fact that support for the Conservatives was hardly merely residual. Nearly 40 per cent of the electorate had voted for the Tories, and Labour had not quite reached the magical 50 per cent that would have allowed them to claim a truly unanswerable mandate. The first-past-the-post system had skewed the results against the Conservatives just as it had against Labour in the 1930s. But the blitzed cities of 1940 had switched massively to Labour. There was a swing of over 18 per cent in London, Portsmouth, Plymouth and Southampton. Even Birmingham, though not as badly blitzed as many other cities, felt guilty about its shamed greatest son, Neville Chamberlain, and swung 23 per cent away from the Conservatives. Many rural constituencies, affected by evacuation among other factors, also swung to Labour.

More likely than not, it was the young voters – those voting for the first time and who had spent the war in the armed forces – who secured Attlee his triumph, even though many of them may have been effectively disenfranchised by the ponderous mechanisms involved in voting while abroad. Among this generation the sense of the failure of the 1930s and the sense of the war as a crusade, seems to have been most acute. Moving from the dole queues into uniform, as the legend has it, the young appear to have been overwhelmingly sure that there must be no return to the bad old days. Yet within five years, Labour was reduced to a five-seat majority and, in 1951, the party was put out of power for thirteen years. It is easy to overstate the significance of 1945, just as it is easy to overstate the supposed new consensus that followed.

7   Refighting the war: Attlee to Blair

From 1945 through to the 1980s, the people's war of 1940 was a constant point of political reference, a moment deemed so sublime as to take it out of the realm of normal historical enquiry entirely. In the 1950s, the summer of 1940 was Mowat's epilogue to *Britain between the Wars*, the moment when the British people found themselves again after the experience of the Depression. The implication was that 1940 was the point when history stopped and the present began. For another fifteen years, there seemed little else for historians to say about this. The official histories largely appeared in the 1950s. Though there were honourable exceptions, many were dry as dust. It was not until the late 1960s that any kind of serious historical debate began on the significance of the war years on the home front. As late as 1975, Paul Addison confirmed the Mowat projection that the war years saw 'Baldwin's consensus' replaced by 'Attlee's consensus', and the assumption appeared to be that that consensus was still with us.[1] In popular political discourse, too, 1940 provided the foundation myth of modern Britain. However, there were always major differences of emphasis within the myth, with widely varying political implications, over the significance of Chamberlain and the 1930s, over the role of the armed forces on the one hand and the common people on the other, over whether the war had been fought for collectivism or for individualism.

The 'lessons' to be learned from 1940 were varied, and they peppered postwar elections. Labour argued successfully in 1945 that the spirit of 1940 should be used to frame action in the future.

> The problems and pressures of the post-war world threaten our security and progress as surely as . . . the Germans threatened them in 1940. We need the spirit of Dunkirk and the Blitz sustained over a period of years. The Labour Party's programme is a practical expression of that spirit applied to the tasks of peace.

In focusing on the failures of the interwar years, they even parodied one of Churchill's most famous pieces of rhetoric from 1940: 'Never was so much injury done to so many by so few.' The experience both of the interwar years and the warfare state showed Labour that the planning of the economy could produce full employment without inflation, that those industries which had failed in the 1930s but which were essential to the economic structure should be taken into public ownership. The wartime expansion of agriculture, the bulk purchase of cheap food from abroad, and public-service restaurants would be continued. Centralized purchasing and price controls would probably be necessary to rebuild the nation's housing stock and to re-plan her shattered cities: 'if that is necessary to get the houses as it was necessary to get the guns and planes, Labour is ready.' There would be a National Health Service and proper social security for all to correct the shabby treatment that had been dealt out to the ill and the unemployed in the long years of Conservative rule. Abroad, a United Nations organization would both establish effective collective security and underpin international prosperity, two areas where international politicians had failed so abysmally in the interwar years.[2]

In 1945, Labour traded on its record in wartime government while the Conservatives traded on Churchill's war leadership. Labour contrasted the actions of the Guilty Men of the 1930s with the state planning that had not only turned the war around in 1940 but also provided the blueprint for the future. For the Conservative leadership in 1945, the lesson of 1940 was primarily an international rather than a domestic one; Britain still had a role in the future in saving the world from tyranny. This international future lay not just with the United Nations but also with the British Empire and Commonwealth, with whom the wartime system of mutual consultation would be extended to cover the whole area of imperial defence. India should move forward to Dominion status. The colonies would be advanced by economic, political and educational means to self-governing status. 'We shall never forget their love and steadfastness when we stood alone against the German Terror.' Finishing the current war and preventing another war was at the forefront of the Conservatives' appeal to the nation in 1945. A call for continued international effort after such a prolonged and costly conflict probably did not appeal overmuch to a war-weary nation. The fact that the international situation was given priority over domestic reconstruction in the manifesto was undoubtedly a major error.

On domestic policy, Tories covered much the same ground as Labour, but with markedly different implications in some areas. To

provide jobs, free enterprise must be given the chance and encouragement to plan ahead, not through state control but through co-
operation between industry and state. In the health service, the
voluntary hospitals would retain their status, and medicine would be
left free in large part, with full play given to the preferences and enterprise of individuals. Education would be developed along the lines
of the 1944 Butler Act, not to produce young adults as cogs in a
standardized machine but responsible and individualized citizens.
True, in rehousing the nation, Conservatives expected to have to
continue to exercise major interventions until the ravages of 1940
had been made good. On the whole, however, since the war had been
fought for freedom, Conservatives warned that the British must not
be led astray by those who would use the necessities of wartime to
impose a permanent huge bureaucratic structure in peacetime, 'reeking
of totalitarianism'.[3] Churchill's ideology of individualism was not without intellectual underpinning in the late 1940s. Von Hayek's *The Road
to Serfdom*, published in 1944, was as much a product of wartime
Western sensibilities as the new popularity of Keynesianism, though
its tenets were not to assume significance until the crisis of Keynesianism in the 1970s.

Though historians and many politicians once argued that there was
little separating the two major political parties in the postwar period
there were actually major variations in their common political discourse, which amounted to very different projections of the future of
Britain. By the 1980s and 1990s when, if there had ever been a consensus, it had clearly collapsed, historians such as José Harris and
Charles Webster questioned the unity of purpose of the postwar
years.[4] Even though, galvanized by the 1945 defeat, Tories began to
listen more carefully to the Tory reform group, and to accept that
they must swim at least part of the way with the tide, there were to
be differences in policy which were more than mere nuances. Both
parties were fully committed to major rehousing, for instance, but a
government commitment to a policy which favours local authority
rented housing will produce a very different society from one which
favours private building for the owner-occupier.

Voting patterns of the postwar period suggest that, far from there
being a consensus, the electorate was very thoroughly divided between
die-hard Labour and die-hard Conservative supporters, but elections
were actually won and lost on the decision of a relatively small minority
of floating voters in marginal constituencies, and it made sense for
political managers to minimize political differences between the parties
in wooing these fickle individuals. For the moment, the Conservative

pursuit of 'freedom' was stymied by the case Labour made that freedom had actually been won by collectivist methods, and that the practicalities of a postwar world in which Britain was virtually bankrupt meant state control would be necessary to husband and develop her slender resources in as efficient a manner as possible. In the development of the Cold War, certainly, Labour and Conservative were in broad agreement. Ernest Bevin had fought against the pacifists in the Labour ranks in the 1930s and was sure, as Labour Foreign Secretary, that Stalin should not be appeased as Hitler had been, because the result would be an even more devastating war. Labour was prepared to hide the funding for the building of Britain's independent nuclear deterrent in the Secret Service estimates, convinced that nothing (not even parliamentary democracy, in this case) must stand in the way of Britain defending herself from the kind of international blackmail that Hitler had used rearmament to achieve in the 1930s. Equally, Churchill pressed his party to accept the terms of the Washington loan recommended by the Labour government, whatever the implications for Britain's freedom of action, given the implications of what Keynes called the 'economic Dunkirk' that faced the nation with the end of Lend-Lease. As in 1940, beyond these areas of agreement to deal with the national emergency, there was a yawning gap between the long-term aspirations of the two parties.

In the face of the most enormous economic difficulties, Labour built its New Jerusalem between 1945 and 1950. With an almost continuous sterling crisis and with the huge problems involved in re-entering the peacetime economy, it was truly a Herculean effort worthy of a group of politicians who had cut their ministerial teeth on the crisis of Dunkirk. Coal, iron and steel, transport and the Bank of England were nationalized, as the conduits through which Keynesian counter-cyclical investment would be channelled to stabilize the economy and to maintain full employment. By 1948, 300,000 new houses were being built annually, to make good the 700,000 houses lost in the war and to rehouse those who had been left in the remaining slums.

An impressive new range of integrated social services was set up, based on the Beveridge principles of comprehensiveness and universality. These were crowned by the National Health Service. Even though Aneurin Bevan had to make major concessions to the medical professionals to gain their acceptance, the result was impressive in its scope and vision; and, in spite of the vicissitudes, the government remained very popular throughout its course. In 1951, Labour actually polled two million more votes than in 1945, achieving its biggest vote ever, but the Conservatives and their allies, with nearly a quarter of a million votes fewer than Labour, scraped home with a small majority. Even though the Tories were to win three general elections in a row in the 1950s, Labour was never far behind, averaging 45 per cent of the poll, 10 per cent more than it averaged in the 1930s. There was no sign, as yet, of the electoral disasters that were to come in the 1980s.

However, continuing strong support for Labour could not disguise the fact that the crusade begun in 1940 had lost some of its zeal by the end of the 1940s. Labour's wartime titans – Bevin, Bevan, Cripps, Dalton and Morrison – were ailing or dying. With the 1945 manifesto largely fulfilled, it was not clear how Labour should move on. There had inevitably been real clashes between Left and Right in implementing the programme in the light of the economic situation: Bevan had quarrelled with Cripps and Gaitskell over the cuts that had been forced on the house-building programme and the NHS so shortly after its inception. In the 1950 and 1951 elections Labour still relied on the memory of the 1930s, and the implied conclusion that Labour's decisive intervention in 1940, and the Party's triumph in 1945, was a victory that must not be given up to those who would go back to the old world. The Tories, 'with their dark past full of bitter memories . . . would take us backward into poverty and insecurity'.[5] The large majority of Labour's election broadcasts in 1950 referred extensively to the interwar slump, and their poster campaigns featured the hunger marchers of the 1930s.[6] But it was already a fading tune: the slogan 'Ask Your Dad' unconsciously, and perhaps harmfully in electoral terms, hinted at a new generational divide. Anyway, with the Conservatives now led by the Tory reformers, it was not at all clear that the party was still dominated by the Guilty Men.

Churchill's return as Prime Minister in 1951 ensured a continuity in foreign policy but a new broom in domestic policy. While maintaining most of the commitments made in economic and social policy by Labour, the Conservatives were able to use the economic boom of the 1950s to sweep away many of the controls that Labour had felt it necessary to maintain. In the Tories' electoral material in the 1950s, there were echoes of Churchill's 1945 warnings against Labour's bureaucratic tendencies, but more successful this time: 'queues, controls, rationing – don't risk it again' proclaimed Tory posters in 1955. The austerity made so necessary by the crisis of 1940 was now part of the past, and the people should be allowed to enjoy the fruits of their victory in a war which had been primarily a crusade for freedom.

The 1930s were to be even less of a burden for the Conservatives when the Grand Old Man himself was succeeded by two men perceived as anti-Chamberlain young Turks from the interwar period, Anthony Eden and Harold Macmillan. Macmillan in particular was determined to show that the people had never had it so good as under the Tories. A series of expansionist budgets through the late 1950s and early 1960s underpinned the new Tory populism. While the balance of payments deficit, virtually wiped out by 1953, reached nearly £800 million by 1964, and in spite of having to go to the International Monetary Fund for loans, Britain enjoyed an unprecedented rise in her standard of living: owner-occupation doubled, car-ownership virtually quadrupled, unemployment was never higher than 2 per cent, and even for the unemployed the dole was pretty generous.

The fridges, washing machines and expensive holidays enjoyed by the few in the 1930s became the expectation of the many. The Tories now had an answer to the 1940 myth of the 1930s that had previously been so damaging for them. By the early 1960s, to 'hark back to the Thirties' could be attacked as an outmoded preference for battles that had long since been fought and decided: for the Conservatives the Left was living in the past if it continued to believe in class war and the socialist crusade. Beveridge and Keynes had reformed capitalism. So, for Conservatives, the People's War had led not to the austere neo-Soviet state favoured by Labour, but to the socially mobile, consumerist, largely carefree society that the flamboyant Macmillan proclaimed, a true partnership between state, production, distribution and exchange. This was the Tory middle way between the 'devil take the hindmost' philosophy of the prewar years and the grim centralism that the crisis of war had made temporarily necessary but which Labour would have institutionalized.[7] Not that such policies were condoned whole-heartedly by all Conservatives: Peter Thorneycroft and Enoch Powell were two strong voices calling for stricter monetary control, for instance. Macmillan, however, was content to enjoy the political consequences of affluence, however short term.

The Left reacted rather uneasily to Tory populism in the 1950s, particularly to the deft way in which Macmillan had stolen their clothes and adapted them – quite literally, in fact, as the traditional working-class cloth cap began to make way for teddy-boy attire on British streets. A better standard of living and a welfare state from cradle to grave had been hard-fought gains in the 1940s, but what shocked many on the Left was the materialist culture that appeared to go with those gains. Paradoxically, many began almost to romanticize the 1930s as a time of commitment and challenge at least, to contrast with what they saw as the slick and self-satisfied triviality of twenty years later. In his seminal text on the new popular culture, *The Uses of Literacy*, Richard Hoggart bemoaned the passing of the old working-class communities, their replacement by the ex-urban estate and the sheet-glass town centre, the replacement of the pub by the coffee bar, and of music-hall by Americanized popular music.[8] In a sense, Hoggart was simply intellectualizing the typical response of the archetypal middle-aged men in the pub to the apparent vapidness of 1950s and 1960s youth: 'to think I fought the Second World War for you lot!' John Osborne's Jimmy Porter in *Look Back in Anger* moaned that there were 'no great causes' any more. Everything had been conceded: no more hunger marches, no more fights with the fascists in the East End, no more appeasement. After 1960, there was not even any further need for conscription. The cities had been rebuilt. But at what cost had this brave new world developed? The new Coventry Cathedral was a modernist nightmare for traditionalists, shorn of the spirituality of the older world. The new cities were clean, brightly lit, smoke-free – and soulless.

The Festival of Britain of 1951 was projected as a symbol of a nation that had come through. On the cusp between Labour and Conservative Britain, it celebrated a nation that looked towards the future – modernist, technological, futuristic, even mystically so – with the Skylon as the Millennium Dome of its time. Yet, for all the forward-looking progressivism of the politics of the time, so much of the dominant popular culture of the period looked backwards. In the symbolic collapse of the older class divisions, Britain sought spiritual solace in revamping traditional forms of national self-projection. Ealing Studios in the immediate postwar years put out a series of gentle, nostalgic comedies at the expense of traditional Britain, half self-mocking and half self-congratulatory. It was a projection that was to resurface in different forms in cinematic representations of the nation over subsequent decades. Ealing had played an active part in the People's War. In *Went the Day Well?*, their wartime propaganda piece dealing with the possibility of invasion, Ealing found their own Guilty Men by casting Lesley Banks and Basil Sydney – two quintessential upper-middle-class heroes of 1930s British film (Banks had played the lead role in *Sanders of the River*) – as traitors. Charles Barr has put forward a gently radical reading of the film. He sees the climactic fight around the mansion house – in which the traitorous squire is shot dead by the vicar's daughter and the democratic community fights off the Germans – as a diagrammatic map of 'England' under attack, exorcizing the ghosts of the past and asserting the social authority of ordinary people.[9]

It is difficult to grade the wartime and postwar heroes of Ealing in specific social terms, except to say that they are not traditional authority figures who are cast more often than not in suspiciously self-regarding roles. The heroes are 'ordinary people' who show resourcefulness, who act individually as well as collectively, and who do not need instructions or leadership. In *Passport to Pimlico* it is the shopocracy who lead the action, those who dominate the community economically as shopkeepers, publicans and the like, but who are recognizably still part of that urban community. They might broadly be defined as 'upper' or 'respectable' working class. But, as often as not, Ealing comedies centre on rural communities resisting the modernizing trends of big business, the state and urbanization, as in *The Maggie, Whiskey Galore* and *The Titfield Thunderbolt*. These are Luddite films in a sense, centring on what were now economically marginal areas of Britain, and making a kind of case for preserving a heritage of pre-industrial, even anti-industrial Britain against the centralizing tendencies of the postwar state. In *Passport to Pimlico*, set in a postwar urban context of bomb-sites and rationing, a *via media* is eventually worked out between the locality and the government. Bomb damage brings to the surface an ancient document which reveals that Pimlico has never been reclaimed from the medieval kingdom of Burgundy, and the borough consequently asserts its independence from Britain. Placed under siege by the national government, Pimlico enjoys sunshine, an end to rationing and a carefree life. There is a downside to this experience, however: the black market runs free and the wartime spivs threaten the community. As Pimlico rejoins Britain at the end of the film, the skies open and the rain pours down, but Pimlico is glad to be back.

The continuation of the themes in British life raised by the experience of 1940 is evident here, but many of the issues take on a modified ideological slant. Resentment at the continued wartime controls in late 1940s Britain work out in what John Ellis has called a 'utopian desire for a self-regulating independent community', but the unwelcome consequence of deregulation is the kind of profiteering associated with individualism which had been criminalized in wartime curbs on excess profits and the black market. The right to be free, for which the country had fought in 1940, is parodied in the film: 'It's because we're English that we are sticking to our right to be Burgundians!', shouts one character in the film. But the community really needs the nation, needs 'Englishness', even more than it needs freedom.[10] Better the boring restraints of a dim, rainy little island, the film finally implies, than the exuberant excesses of continentalism.

Ealing's chief, Michael Balcon, quite consciously saw the role of the studio as the projection of Britain, in much the same way as John Reith had seen the role of the BBC in the prewar years. Known as 'the studio with the team spirit', Ealing was to become almost as synomous with Britain as Hollywood was with America, though on a much smaller scale and for a much shorter period, of course. It was an insular and self-deprecating world that Ealing constructed, which projected British values as a stubborn, virtually myopic, patriotic individualism (recalling David Low's lone soldier in 1940 shouting across the Channel, 'Very well, alone!'), a hatred for authoritarianism and a preference for consensus and the popular will ('the Dunkirk Spirit'), but also a preference for the tried and the tested rather than the new. If Britain had stood the test in 1940 when all others failed, why should the values that underpinned the nation be called into question now?

In television, too, which actually did so much to undermine the role of cinema as the prime social habit in the 1950s, the theme of community was expanded and developed. *Dixon of Dock Green*, one of the longest running and most successful of all BBC television productions, resurrected PC George Dixon, shot dead in the Ealing film *The Blue Lamp* by a vicious thug played by the young Dirk Bogarde. Dixon, the gentle community policeman, built on the new image of policing that had developed during the emergency of the early war years. He certainly was not the agent of social control of the proletarian novels of the 1930s, nor even the heroic baton-wielding peacekeeper in the conflict between Left and Right extremists in the East End. Dixon was portrayed as a sort of social worker rather than an agent of the law as such. A word in the ear of a parent was normally enough to keep a potential hooligan on the straight and narrow, though investigation often revealed a family social problem which, once sorted out, allowed Dixon to deliver his habitual final homily on the sort of little tragedies that affected people less fortunate than ourselves. This was a community cured of its prewar grimness by the experience of the war and by welfarism. Social misfortune was not the lot of the many any more but of the few, and might well be due to personal inadequacy, but it was up to the agents of the many – the policeman and the social worker – to help those few.

During the 1960s, however, *Dixon* visibly cracked as a vehicle for the projection of policing. Andy Crawford, Dixon's son-in-law in the CID (even policing was a family business), became a more hard-nosed detective, and consequently his marriage broke up. While newer series did not overlook the social aspect of policing, they featured more ebullient, dedicated criminal catchers such as Barlow, paving the way for the desocialized and brutalized professionals who were to feature in the police series of the 1970s and beyond. By that time, whatever remained of the wartime consensus had broken down. The perceived crisis of law and order, even more than economic chaos and industrial strife, was fashioning a new political agenda. Yet the community story retained a huge popular following. *Coronation Street* began in the early 1960s, initially as a televisual response to New Wave in the cinema, but quickly transforming itself into a cosy, nostalgic and sentimental look at the communities occupying the back-to-back housing built in the Edwardian period. It is no coincidence that this was the period when the last of those estates which had survived the Blitz were being pulled down. During the 1980s, the BBC responded to the huge success of *Coronation Street* with *EastEnders*, supposedly a more realistic soap than its chief rival. *EastEnders* concentrated on the life of the community which, more than any other, had been heroicized by the Blitz. The opening title sequence, an aerial view of the bend in the Thames, worked an instant historical connection for anyone who has ever picked up a picture book on the Blitz and seen the ubiquitous wartime photographs of Luftwaffe bombers over exactly the same bend in the river.

This is not to say that the community story originates with the Blitz: clearly, it has a much longer history in popular literature and film. But it was the Blitz which made the community story a principal element in the interior monologue of the nation, harking back to a time when life was tougher but people showed their best sides. They portray a matri- archal world dominated by hard-pressed but gritty women, pitted against 'outsiders' – invariably men, or at least, patriarchal forces – who threaten their property, their families and their way of life. Though characters such as Dot Cotton and Ethel, who habitually dropped references to the experience of the war in *EastEnders*, have been replaced by younger characters with more 'contemporary' attitudes and problems, the setting remains essentially that of the pub-centred 1930s–40s working-class communities, virtually all of which have either been pulled down or gentrified in the intervening years.

But to suggest that postwar popular culture was solely concerned with the notion of a traditional community mythicized by the Blitz would clearly be wrong. While one may trace a line of continuity, albeit indirect, between wartime projections of the home front and 1990s soap opera, there occurred a quite marked disjuncture in the presentation of the military side of the war. During the war, films about the fighting were relatively few and far between. Documentaries

Figure 9 Reach for the Sky – 'Yours Forever'. Rank Video offers you a portion of British heritage in their video of the 1956 film of the role played by Douglas Bader in the Battle of Britain, a pilot even more disadvantaged than most by the fact that he was disabled. © Rank Video.

of victories, such as *Desert Victory* and *The Battle of Stalingrad*, made good propaganda and were very popular, but feature-film makers were understandably reticent about telling stories of the fighting to audiences whose sons and husbands were out there fighting, especially when it was not going too well. Apart from *The First of the Few*, wartime films about the fighting front tended to be a variation on the 'People's War' theme for the home front. They concentrated on the training of disparate recruits into a people's army in *The Way Ahead*, for example, or on the warship as symbol of the national family militant, as it were, in *In Which We Serve*. *San Demetrio, London* and *Western Approaches* concentrated on ordinary people's extraordinary bravery as merchant mariners bringing food and supplies essential for the survival of Britain. But during the 1950s and early 1960s, films of the derring-do of the armed forces in the recent war were not only legion, they also regularly topped the box-office returns in Britain. Partly, of course, this was safe material now that the war was over and won; but they also offered an alternative ideological focus for presentation of the war as a whole, picking up on the themes of *The First of the Few*, itself rather marginalized and unusual during the war itself.

Angels One Five was among the first, in 1952, shot in the semi-documentary style that became so familiar to the genre. Underplayed to the point of moroseness by its star, Jack Hawkins, it was a grim story of British reserve and resolve triumphing over impossible odds in the Battle of Britain. The subsequent years found Hawkins – the rugged and reserved British male *par excellence* – transferred to the Royal Navy for *The Cruel Sea,* another huge box-office success in Britain in the year of the Coronation. *The Dam Busters* followed in 1955, which featured Richard Todd's famous moment of stifled mourning at the death of his pet Labrador dog just before the raid. In 1956, *Reach for the Sky* told the story of Douglas Bader, the legendary Battle of Britain pilot who faced even more overwhelming odds than most in the fact that he had lost both legs. All of these films, as is true of the war film genre more generally, are about men proving their masculinity. Family life and femininity are marginalized in pursuit of the quest.

It is not that these British films of the 1950s glorify war, which is pictured as a grim and gruelling business. The war, after all, did not need to be justified; the fight against Hitler was already overwhelmingly accepted in the country as a just war; but what underlies all these films is, first, a sense of the particularly challenging circumstances in which Britain had been placed by the fall of the whole of mainland Western Europe in 1940, and, second, a sense that only the British male character could have seen it through. There to the south and east is the mass of Europe, darkened and fortified by Nazism. There to the west is the grey Atlantic, bristling with U-boats. In the centre is the little, lonely, offshore island. The quest is that much more impressive, and the mission that much more heroic, for the grim, quiet way in which it is pursued. It is the collapse of Europe which made the task of the fighter pilots in the Battle of Britain so difficult; it is also the reason why bomber pilots had to fly many hours at night at low level through enemy-occupied territory to reach significant targets; it is this also that made the Atlantic Ocean such a cruel fighting ground for the convoy escorts. There is no room for amateurishness in meeting such a challenge, but there is certainly room for traditional male British stiff upper lips and self-sacrificing determination. In fact, these films imply, no other qualities could have won in such a desperate situation.

These are the heroes of Churchill's war, of the few rather than the many, who impose their presence on British popular culture in the 1950s as much as do the values of the People's War. In one very obvious sense, these are not really opposed views of the war, but complementary ones. Solid community spirit could not have won the war without the armed forces, any more than the armed forces could have won the war without arms production from the home front, but they are very different projections of the war. They do not meet up, but exist in the different worlds of matriarchy and patriarchy. I have no doubt that it was pure coincidence that these war films began to be made when the Conservatives returned to office, but the retirement of Churchill in 1955 no doubt touched a public nerve and gave them an added appeal. Certainly, Churchill's death in 1965 did so once again.

The stolid and serious-minded 1969 film *The Battle of Britain* stands as a prime cinematic tribute to the Great Man and his particular myth of 1940. In its reverential treatment of its subject matter, its budget and its all-star cast, the film is in many ways out of sorts with the cultural climate of the 1960s, when many cinematic historical dramas called into question the gloriousness of Britain's past. The Battle of Britain was clearly not yet subject matter for cinematic revision. Four years after Churchill's death, there is a cameo appearance of a Churchill look-alike in the background in Fighter Command's Control Room, watching the plots on the map table at the most dangerous moment of the whole battle. 'Winston would pick on a day like this to turn up', comments one officer with a grim smile. Keith Park is pictured talking to Churchill, then walking over to the Controller and asking, 'Is everything up?' 'Yes, sir.' 'Reserves?' 'None.' 'That's what I've just told the Prime Minister.'[11] There is gravitas and reserve for you.

In fact, neither gravitas nor reserve were particularly in vogue by the time the film was made. By the late 1960s there were clear signs that Keynesianism was falling apart, as inflation gathered momentum and the trade balance soared. For the Left, the mixed economy established with nationalization after 1945 had only been a step on the road to the socialist economy anyway, but Labour revisionists such as Anthony Crosland and Richard Crossman were suggesting that the traditional socialist goals were outmoded. Clause IV of the Labour Constitution, for instance, had been conceived at the end of the Great War and had nothing to do with the realities of life in the postwar world. If the mixed economy were all that was needed, then Labour's historic mission had presumably been largely completed with the political coup of 1940 and the bloodless revolution of 1945.

The turbulent years of the Wilson government of the second half of the 1960s saw the Left gather itself for a new assault on the structure, not content any longer to bask in the light of the gains made in a war that had ended a quarter of a century previously. Angus Calder's history of the home front between 1939 and 1945, *The People's War*, published in 1969, did not underestimate the huge sacrifices that had been made by the British in the Second World War, and he paid tribute to the Labour leaders who had pulled the country through, but his reckoning on the longer-term gains made by Labour was a pretty bitter one. By the 1960s, he claimed, one Briton in seven lived below the National Assistance minimum standard of living, and the number was growing. Unemployment had not been abolished but stabilized at around half a million: 'for reasons which economists and other plump men in expensive suits would never tire of explaining, the prosperity of the many would necessitate the idleness of the few'.[12] The great opportunity, in other words, had been wasted. For the Right, the conclusions from the vantage point of the late 1960s were very different. The great crusade was once again to roll back the tide of state intervention, to free the people from the kind of central direction that could only be justified in emergencies such as that of 1940. Edward Heath's government came into power in 1970 committed to rolling back the tide of increased taxation. The recessionary effects of the first monetarist budgets soon changed the government's mind. By 1972, unemployment was approaching one million, and there were still enough memories of the 1930s around, focused through the prism of the war years, to make that a politically frightening total. Meanwhile, the effects of devaluation pushed the trade deficit over £1 billion, and the Middle East oil crisis threatened worse to come. Heath did decide to stay on course with his anti-trade union policy, taking on the miners' strike with a three-day week and then a general election on the issue of who ruled the country. The fact that he lost that election laid him open to a devastating attack from the Right of his own party, that he had sold out the monetarist cause on which he had been elected. His replacement as leader by Margaret Thatcher was not at the time recognized as the major change it was to be, since the majority of commentators assumed that Thatcher would mellow and move to the centre in time. Power, it was believed, would force her to take the pragmatic line, just as it had in Heath's case earlier in the decade. One should not overestimate the extent of the Thatcher revolution that followed. Much was to remain intact from the postwar settlement, if only because it proved so difficult to deconstruct. Nevertheless the new rhetoric of politics signalled that the lady was not for turning, and the era which took it as read that state intervention was a good thing had ended.

It was not Thatcher's election in 1979 that was the real turning point, however, but her election to a second term in 1983. Opinion polls after 1979 suggested that Thatcher's was the most unpopular government since the war. The odds were that Labour would probably win the next election, though perhaps with only a small majority, and that Keynesian methods would return. What really confirmed the new course was the Falklands War, which wholly realigned the myths of 1940. Lucy Noakes has examined, in a telling argument, the way in which gender constructions of the Second World War underlay representations of what was being played out in the South Atlantic.[13] In fact, there are a number of different ways in which the 1940s and subsequent reformulations of the war resonate through the Falklands conflict and its consequences. Britain was fighting a dictator again, and alone. A BBC reporter, Brian Hanrihan, watched as the new 'few' went to work again, this time not from green English airfields but from the grey deck of an aircraft carrier, almost as if the story of *Angels One Five* and *The Dam Busters* had been filmed on the set of *The Cruel Sea*. Like a fretful bomber or fighter commander in a film from thirty years previously, Hanrihan counted them all out and counted them back in. Exocet missiles doodle-bugged into the British fleet.

As HMS Coventry and the Atlantic Conveyor were sunk, the *Sun* headlined: 'Our Darkest Hour.' I remember being affected by this headline when I first saw it at my local newsagent. It struck a chord, but I still find it hard to pin down. The direct reference is of course to the saying, 'the darkest hour is just before dawn', but that was not how it resonated with me. It seems to me a choice of words only fully understandable in a country culturally attuned to the popular memory of the 'finest hour'.[14] Michael Foot, Leader of the Opposition and co-writer of *Guilty Men* over forty years previously, could not avoid the parallels. He spoke of the need 'to ensure that foul and brutal aggression does not succeed in the world', while Douglas Jay suggested that the Foreign Office had been 'saturated with the spirit of appeasement' in not foreseeing the crisis.[15] This time the only threat to the home front was internal, in the shape of Arthur Scargill and the National Union of Mineworkers. The miners had been a *bête noire* of the Conservatives since the General Strike in 1926, but a particular edge had been added to the friction by the part they had played in the more recent defeat of the Heath government.

The fifth column threat in 1940, the possibility that blackshirts and aliens might disrupt Britain's ability to resist, had been largely overridden by the sentiments of the People's War. This time there was no People's War, just a professional few yomping across small islands in the South Atlantic. In a desperate attempt to re-appropriate the legacy of 1940, the Labour Party produced an election handbill that featured one of the most iconographic photographs of the unemployment of the 1930s. Underneath were the words: 'The Bad Days are Back. This General Election is the past versus the future. As Labour rebuilt Britain after the last war, so we are now ready to rebuild Britain after Tory destruction.' It was indeed the past versus the future, but not in quite the way that Michael Foot had hoped. The result of the 1983 General Election served notice that the 1940s now meant something quite different. Labour was subsequently to split as it lost the unifying moral high ground that the 'People's War' had bequeathed the party. In the ensuing miners' strike, Mrs Thatcher turned her full patriotic wrath on the dictators at home, having despatched the dictator abroad. In the summer of 1984, of all years, Arthur Scargill and the leadership of the National Union of Mineworkers were projected as 'the enemy within', just as dangerous to democracy as Galtieri and the Argentinean Junta, and just as necessary to defeat.

Between the beginning of the Falklands War in 1982 and the defeat of the miners' strike in 1985, the domestic political meaning of 1940 was effectively rewritten: 1982 was the 1940 of the late century, 1983 its 1945, and the ensuing two years saw the attempt at the legislative and cultural undermining of the postwar domestic settlement. Thatcherism found new Guilty Men – among the politicians of the 1960s and 1970s, now projected as a decadent couple of decades which had championed libertarianism in morality and profligacy in economics, resulting in the rapid decline of Britain. The 1930s, by contrast, began to get a better press. Norman Tebbitt proclaimed that when his father had been unemployed between the wars, he had not expected to sit back and let the state take the burden; he had 'got on his bike' and searched for a job.

Historians had already been revising their views on the interwar years. In *The Slump*, first published in 1977 and attracting a great deal of attention in the press at the time for its iconoclasm, John Stevenson and Chris Cook summarized and developed the revisionist case on the interwar years that had begun to appear in academic journals over the previous years. The authors did not deny that there was widespread poverty between the wars, but concentrated instead on the implications of what they saw as the more important fact that most people were better off than they had ever been before during that period. The threat from the communists and the blackshirts had been overemphasized in the traditional picture, they argued, because they were never more than the interests of a small minority in a country which had voted overwhelmingly for the mainstream parties. The beginnings of the consumer revolution in the 1930s had made most people relatively happy with the way things were, and even the worse-off had been able to benefit from a generous social policy. The National governments, far from being Guilty Men in domestic policy at least, had provided stable administration and a feeling of security in a period of deep international uncertainty.[16] Without the failures of appeasement, the National government might have continued to command the confidence of the people.

The implication was that the new affluence that had begun in the 1930s was just as important for the future as the legacy of mass unemployment. While the latter had been seized upon by the Left, in 1940 and beyond, as the rationale for the welfare state, affluence had actually been the result of economic changes that had begun before 1940 and was just as important in shaping the future of Britain. Affluence indeed was basic to welfarism; government profligacy had produced that politics of resentment among the majority of 'haves' at the cost of maintaining the minority of 'have-nots'. The result was Thatcherism, a return to the principles of sound finance that had characterized the interwar years, and a reliance on free enterprise to do what the state had conspicuously and expensively proved itself incapable of doing in the postwar years. By 1999, though now in Opposition, the Conservatives even toyed with the idea of a Balanced Budget Act to outlaw deficit budgeting, so far had the principles of sound finance been revamped.

Just as the Conservatives had fallen in behind a Tory reform view of welfarism after the election defeats of 1945 and 1950, so Labour fell in behind the New Labour view of the future after the electoral disasters that had given the Conservatives an unprecedented four terms in office. In so doing, Labour pitched its tents further to the right than had ever before been the case, having no choice but to fight on the new terrain that Thatcherism had mapped out. If Thatcherism in the 1980s fatally undermined the unsteady Keynes–Beveridge axis, which was conceived in the crisis of 1940 and born in the 1945 General Election, Blairism created new political space for the Centre–Left in Britain. Celebrating one hundred years of the Labour Party, and with the millennium around the corner, Tony Blair offered a new crusade against 'the forces of conservatism', forces which now ranged, it seemed, from those traditionalists who supported fox-hunting on the one hand to, on the other, those public sector workers, fearful of change, who had traditionally supported Old Labour.[17] Blair seemed to have moved Labour from 'outmoded' socialism, which still 'harked back to the Thirties', to something akin to progressivism. New Labour helped the heirs of Thatcher to redefine the terms of engagement of British politics, in positing for itself a belief in the power of government not to control but to regulate advanced capitalism for the public good, irrespective of particularist class loyalties. Thus 1940, for so long the birthday of 'contemporary Britain', has itself passed into history, a moment that moulded the present but which no longer underpins it.

Having passed into history, however, 1940 is still open to interpretation in mapping the path between the past and the present. Reacting angrily to Tony Blair's attack on the 'forces of conservatism', William Hague declared himself proud to be in the tradition of those forces:

> Winston Churchill and the British people, hand in hand, as we stood alone and saved Europe from tyranny. Rab Butler and the British people, hand in hand, as we extended free education and brought opportunity to millions of children. Harold Macmillan and the British people, hand in hand, as we brought prosperity to the cold, grey post-war era. Margaret Thatcher and John Major and the British people, hand in hand, as we freed the nation from state intervention.[18]

It is an interesting list, an interesting view of the Tory journey from 1940 to the present. It not only keeps the ghost of Churchill alive and links it with the Iron Lady, but it also relates that link to Tory reform. It thus seeks to appropriate the legacy of the People's War to the central Tory agendum to 'set the people free' through prosperity rather than to chain them in welfare. But it was in attitudes towards Britain's position in the world, particularly in relation to developments in Europe and their consequences for British freedom of action, that the myths of 1940 proved most divisive, most convoluted and long lasting.

8 America, Europe and the world

In 1983, Gallup conducted a poll for the *Sunday Telegraph* on British attitudes to Europe. It was discovered that more than one in four believed Germany to be Britain's best friend in Europe, compared with more than one in ten in 1968. France had emerged as second favourite, but only of fewer than one in ten. Erstwhile favourites such as Holland and Denmark had fallen back. To this extent, the British appear to have got used to the realities of Europe in the here and now, no longer heroicizing the gallant little resisters of the war days. However, when asked which European country they would rather live in if they could not live in Britain, more preferred France and Switzerland to Germany. The most interesting findings referred to travel in Europe. More than half the respondents had visited France by 1983, compared with one in three in 1968. The number of people who had visited Spain had tripled. In spite of the enormous development in continental travel, however, British linguistic skills had improved hardly at all; only 13 per cent could speak French and a mere 6 per cent could speak German.[1]

The *Sunday Telegraph* commented that it was remarkable that Germany had been transformed from pariah nation to 'best friend in Europe' in under forty years. Perhaps the figures suggested something a little subtler, a respect for the Germans and a willingness to do business with them as the economic power of Europe, but not a people with whom you could relax or befriend. Europe has always been two very different things for Britain since the war: on the one hand an economic community but, on the other, a holiday community, and the countries involved in each community have tended to be different. Looking at these results, the *Sunday Telegraph* bemoaned the distaste among some sections of the British public for the American connection. The Left was the particular target here. An editorial noted that 'in Moscow, of all places, Mr Scargill has been blithely directing his venom against

President Reagan (although characteristically he saved some of it for his own elected government).'[2] Making friends with old enemies was one thing, the newspaper implied, but disavowing old friends was quite another.

For the larger part of the period since the war, the implications of 1940 have deeply affected British attitudes to the outside world: 1940 confirmed Britain's difference from the rest of Europe, while her utter reliance on the USA would be interpreted by many as a 'special relationship' with another 'Anglo-Saxon' people. Most British politicians appear to have believed that their nation retained a unique freedom of action, and that 1940 had given her a moral authority to play a major part in the direction of world affairs. European integration, for example, was 'for them, but not for us', in Churchill's phrase. First of all, European integration was a way of solving the problem of the interwar years. The Briand Plan of 1929 had been designed to build on the steel cartel of 1926 between France, Germany, Belgium and Luxemburg. Understanding that economic co-operation was a particularly important part of international understanding, the Briand Plan was significant for its willingness to give up at least some national sovereignty in a bid to achieve even larger national goals, namely a lasting peace, without which France might be permanently in danger from German revanchism. Although Gustav Stresemann was prepared to talk on such issues, the scheme died with the economic recession, and with the death of Stresemann himself.

The British, for their part, were largely unimpressed from the start. Britain still relied on the export of heavy industrial products, the market for which did not seem strong in Europe. In fact, British trade with Europe actually fell by 20 per cent between 1913 and 1939.[3] This simply reinforced British interest in trade with those underdeveloped nations which were still prepared to buy such material. In fact, the terms of trade and the development of Japanese competition in such areas as textiles meant that the Empire and Commonwealth was nowhere near the safe market Britain assumed it to be. Irrespective of this, the British still preferred free trade to the idea of regional trading blocs. Frankly, the Briand Plan stood little chance of success, with or without British support, but at least Briand perceived the important point that defending national interests need not always imply aggression, particularly when faced with the complicated issues of nationality in such a crowded continent.[4]

With the onset of the depression, any ideas of economic co-operation disappeared as nationalism grew rampant. The British retreated into imperial preference and the Sterling area. But the idea of a federal

Europe did not entirely fall on deaf ears in Britain. Archbishop Temple and Lord Lothian were both important converts among the elite. The support for such an idea grew, if only with the benefit of hindsight, once Britain had been excluded entirely from the European mainland by the fall of Western Europe and the proclamation of the Nazi New Order. The clear failure of appeasement, again with the benefit of hindsight, convinced the Foreign Office that a much more definite commitment to Europe must be made once the current conflict was over. The offer of a permanent union with France was made in the summer of 1940 largely as a panic reaction to try to keep France in the war, but it was part of a wider understanding that Britain could no longer simply assume that European affairs had nothing to do with her, beyond the need to maintain a balance of power. The emergence of Germany as a major power in the centre of Europe had undermined entirely the assumption that Britain could effortlessly pull the European puppet strings while exploiting her world trade. In 1940, union was, anyway, rejected by a French Cabinet which believed that Nazi victory was inevitable and who assumed that the British would simply use the legislation to take over the French empire.

The circumstances of the French campaign in 1940 underlined nationalist prejudices in both countries. To xenophobes in Britain, the rapid defeat of France simply confirmed French effeminacy, while for French patriots the self-seeking strategy of the British seemingly confirmed the traditional perfidy of the Anglo-Saxons. Incipient French Anglophobia was deftly played on by the contemporary Nazi taunt that Britain would fight to the last Frenchman. In the awful shock and humiliation of defeat, French sensibilities were hardly assuaged by the action of the British in sinking the French fleet, however necessary that may have been to prevent it from falling into the hands of the Germans. General Charles de Gaulle, ever a French nationalist but even more so faced with the humiliating need to accept British hospitality after the defeat, proved a prickly presence in London, demanding an advisory role in any decisions taken which involved the French mainland. Churchill described the symbol of the Free French, the Cross of Lorraine, as the second cross he had to bear.

Yet there was some strong support from other governments in exile, for example Holland and Belgium, for Britain to organize some form of Western bloc after the war as a united front if Germany should attempt to cut loose again. The Foreign Office also believed that it would be important for Britain to take a lead in West European affairs, partly to organize the defence in depth that had been so lacking in 1940, partly to ensure that Britain would maintain a significant leadership role in a world that would otherwise be dominated by the Soviet Union and the United States.[5] De Gaulle, however, would only consider close involvement with the British if they agreed to help impose a harsh peace on Germany and to respect French colonial interests in the Middle East. On neither issue were the British prepared to concede.

Though many accepted the need to take a political lead on the Continent for geopolitical reasons in the wake of 1940, there was little sympathy in Britain for closer economic links with the European mainland. Both the Treasury and the Board of Trade argued that Britain should seek to preserve her independence, to continue with her world-trading tradition and develop her links with the Commonwealth. Britain would continue to be primarily a global power, even if she should involve herself more closely at least in the diplomacy of Europe. Ernest Bevin as Foreign Secretary did show some passing interest in a customs union in Western Europe to strengthen any alliance system that developed, and to fortify the postwar world against communist influence, but political leadership was his priority, not economic co-operation. Britain also assumed in the immediate postwar period that free-trading America would not take kindly to the idea of Europe forming a protectionist bloc. However, in 1947, emerging worries about the Soviets played their part in the development of the Marshal Plan, the effects of which split Europe in two and made it clear that the Americans were to be keen supporters of unity in Western Europe.

The effects were to be double-edged for Britain. On the one hand, she was glad of American aid and thankful for the implication of continued American support. On the other hand, there was the clear implication that Britain should involve herself more thoroughly in Europe than she would wish. Bevin was miffed that Britain was to be treated as 'just another European country'.[6] Clearly, Britain would never be strong enough to stand on her own as a 'third force' in the world. The developing pressures of the Cold War meant inevitably that Britain would tie herself to the American ship, but, if she could emerge as a leader of Europe as well as of the Commonwealth, she could perform an important, independent role as diplomatic bridge between America, Europe and many of the emerging nations of the world. Thus the aim of British European policy should be to create a Western union, backed by the Commonwealth, to develop British power and influence to equal that of the USA and the Soviet Union. As the European survivor of 1940, the leadership of Europe was assumed to be Britain's for the asking. But in a single week in February 1947, in deep financial crisis, the weaknesses of Britain's global position became clear with three momentous announcements: first, that Britain would have to hand back the Palestinian problem unsolved to the United Nations; second, that she could no longer afford to aid the Greeks and the Turks against communism; and third, that she would leave India, and whatever problems remained, within fourteen months.

The Brussels Pact of March 1948 nevertheless carried British European aims forward. Britain and France joined with the Low Countries in a military pact that also looked forward to financial, cultural and other forms of co-operation. Belgium, Holland and Luxemburg had already formed their customs union, and the setting up of the Organisation for European Economic Co-operation to supervise the Marshall Aid programme presaged greater things in the development of common policies and co-operation. There was close cross-party agreement on these points. Churchill spoke grandly of a United States of Europe but it is pretty clear that though he expected Britain to be interested in this development, Britain would not actually be part of it. Neither Conservatives nor Labour were prepared to develop European institutions that would threaten British national sovereignty. The aim was to lead Europe, not to be subsumed into it. In particular, the British became alarmed at the wilder talk that began to develop in Europe about the likelihood of a European Assembly, with possibly federalist implications. But it was the establishment of a West German government, reviving as it did so many European and particularly French fears of the past, which began to force the issue of integration, which the British were consequently unable to control.[7]

The belief that only the British could act as broker between France and Germany – given their history of antagonism – was rudely undermined when the Schumann Plan proved that those two countries could come to mutually beneficial agreements. France was anxious to tie the new West German state into an economic partnership that would make military aggression virtually impossible. West Germany was similarly anxious to tie herself to the liberal democracies, to put Nazism firmly in the past and to encourage mutual protection against the mighty monolithic alliance developing beyond her eastern frontier. This was a scheme that did not even need British participation, let alone British leadership, and the French had caught the British on the hop. Indeed, Bevin was not even informed of the plan before it was announced. The French called a conference for anyone considering joining the scheme but insisted that it stood or fell on the principle of supranationalism, a high authority that would control the steel and coal industries of all participating members. The French must have known that the British could never join such a scheme. Britain had the largest coal and steel industries in Europe, and they had just been nationalized by a government unlikely to quickly surrender its authority in such key areas for the reconstruction of the national economy. In addition, Britain still traded much more extensively with the rest of the world than with Europe. This was a decisive moment. It ensured that the pace of European union would henceforth be dictated by the French and Germans in consort, with the British caught between the wish to lead and an unwillingness to become directly embroiled.

The formation of the European Coal and Steel Community (ECSC) paved the way for further schemes of integration. French worries about German rearmament led the 'Six', those who joined the ECSC, to consider a federal military force, a European Defence Community (EDC). In the end, in August 1954, even the French Assembly rejected this, but not before Britain had rushed to keep up by signing a treaty of association with the EDC. With the demise of the new French scheme, the British were able to put forward a more successful case for an inter-governmental rather than a federal scheme, a widening of the Brussels Pact to include West Germany and Italy, with West Germany joining NATO as a sovereign state.[8] It was a fairly minor victory, but it kept alive the British hope that Europe, as in the past, would be too divided to federate and would come to see the sense of Britain's less involved solutions.

Britain associated herself with the work of the Spaak Committee, aware that she would suffer if a common market were set up in Europe from which she was excluded, but withdrew from the work of the Committee before it reported, thus effectively ruling herself out of entry to the European Economic Community (EEC). Most British politicians assumed that the idea would fail anyway, like the EDC before it. The government decided on an alternative plan in an attempt to seize the initiative, a European Free Trade Area (EFTA) rather than a customs union. This was widely interpreted in France as an attempt to scotch the EEC, and it consequently strengthened rather than weakened French resolve. By March 1957, the Treaty of Rome had been signed while the EFTA proposal existed only on paper. Severely humiliated by the Suez crisis a year previously, Britain's dream of becoming the leader of a third force in the world was driven severely off-course. The problems were simply that leadership was impossible without membership, and that Europe did not need nor want British leadership anyway. Britain's assumption was that her survival in 1940 showed her fitness to lead, whereas, in fact, it was her very different experience of 1940 that isolated her from Europe.

The year 1940 had seemed to confirm the strength of Britain but utterly destroyed any such self-belief in the rest of Europe. Britain had adapted and changed in 1940 and, buoyed up by American money and hardware, had survived the war. But being on the right side in 1945 did not mean that Britain had won the war, though she continued to behave as though she had. Ernest Bevin remarked in 1947 that 'His Majesty's Government do not accept the view . . . that we have ceased to be a great power. . . . The very fact that we have fought so hard for liberty, and paid such a price, warrants our retaining this position; and indeed it places a duty upon us to continue to retain it.' Jean Monnet saw British attitudes as 'the price of victory the illusion that you could maintain what you had, without change'.[9] Konrad Adenauer said that Britain was 'like a rich man who had lost all his property but does not realize it'.[10]

Other European countries saw the need fundamentally to rethink their attitude towards the rest of the world. After the two biggest wars in history, in which many millions of their inhabitants had died, most of the countries of mainland Western Europe decided that national sovereignty was not the be-all and end-all of a nation's existence, that it was possible to retain some notion of national identity but that it was essential to give something of that identity up to a wider European identity if peace and sanity were to prevail. Certainly, there was wounded pride in France, and this undoubtedly contributed to a sense that Britain should be denied the leadership of Europe; but Britain's assumption that she could ever provide that leadership was based on an overestimate of just what 1940 had achieved for Britain. Anthony Eden seemed determined in 1956 that Britain's prewar reputation for appeasement demanded a forthright response to the 'new Hitler', Gemal Abdul Nasser. British actions in the Middle East actually led to a humiliation, if anything even worse than that of Munich. Not only was the Suez Canal not saved, but the crisis wholly undermined any effective Western response to Soviet moves in Hungary; at the same time, the British were deflected from giving due attention to crucial developments in Europe.

Suez undermined any hopes that the special relationship with America gave Britain any particular privileges in the world. Yet it worked to prompt the British to wish to repair and strengthen the American alliance, whereas for France it worked to propel her more quickly into the EEC. The EEC was not, anyway, as federalist in its approach as the ECSC had been, whatever the British fears. The Council of Ministers ensured that national interests rather than a supranational authority would prevail. While Britain continued with the EFTA scheme, attempting to maintain her global role by protecting her Commonwealth trade links, it was soon clear that the EEC countries would have no real benefits in associating with such a scheme. This effectively left the EFTA scheme dead in the water, since it provided nowhere near a big enough market to assure British trade in the future.

Europe became a more hostile environment when the collapse of the Fourth Republic in France brought de Gaulle back to power. On the one hand, this undercut British fears of a federalist future in Europe; de Gaulle was known to favour a *Europe de patries* rather than a United States of Europe. On the other hand, the war years had made de Gaulle no friend of Britain, and he was deeply suspicious of Britain's interest in Europe. Immediately adopting an aggressive policy, de Gaulle made it clear that the leadership of Europe was with France, working in close association with the Federal Republic of Germany (FRG). With the Americans pushing Britain to take a more active role, Harold Macmillan approached the decision to apply for entry to the EEC with some trepidation, aware that this American wish was one very good reason why Britain might find application difficult.

The negotiating stance was not helped by an opinion poll which showed that two-thirds of Britons did not even know which European network Britain was involved with, the EFTA or the EEC, or got the answer wrong.[11] Perhaps de Gaulle always intended to use his veto to block British entry, but it was the Nassau Agreement which gave him the best possible excuse. Macmillan pleaded successfully with President Kennedy to allow Britain to have Polaris, so that Britain could at least pretend to be an independent nuclear power. This was hardly calculated to ease French worries that Britain was more interested in maintaining world power status than in the future of Europe, particularly when the French were involved in projecting their own nuclear capability as being quite independent from that of the United States.[12]

De Gaulle's veto was another humiliating blow for Britain, so soon after the Suez crisis had so cruelly displayed her collapse as a great power on the world stage. Not only did Europe not want British leadership, she would not even let her in. In fact, the rest of the Six would probably have been happy for Britain to join, but they were not prepared to upset France in the process. In the ensuing months, the Macmillan government collapsed in tatters as foreign disaster was followed by murky domestic political scandals. Yet the incoming Labour government of Harold Wilson was no more direct or rational in its European policy. Like many on the Conservative benches, Hugh Gaitskell had favoured the Commonwealth connection over the European one, and had worried about surrendering control of economic policy when such controls had become central to Labour's concept of social planning. Many on the Left of the party saw the EEC as a 'capitalist club'. But the leading pro-marketeers, George Brown and Michael Stewart, were convinced that it was the only way of protecting the British future now that Commonwealth trade was declining, trade with Europe increasing, and the Americans unwilling to offer a lifeline for independence. De Gaulle still stood in the way.

Astute politician though he was, Wilson was quite unable to charm and manipulate the formidable old French warhorse, who likened Wilson to the kind of politician who had brought down the Fourth Republic. Wilson played a canny game, unwilling to commit the government to try again so soon after the French veto and before the 1966 election gave him a workable majority. Though he managed to hold the Party together in preparing for a second application, this was probably only because the anti-marketeers were fairly certain that de Gaulle would do their work for them. Wilson refused to devalue the pound voluntarily to prepare the economy for Europe, so that when the government was forced to devalue involuntarily, de Gaulle was ready to deliver a second major rebuff. Not only was Britain still seen as an American Trojan Horse, she was still not European enough in her outlook, and now her economy looked too weak to take the strain of entry.[13] Effectively, the power relationship between Britain and France had been reversed over little more than a quarter of a century.

Thus did de Gaulle wreak his revenge for the slights inflicted on his country in 1940. The French myth of 1940, after all, was as deep-seated and pervasive as the British version across the Channel. France had effectively seized the leadership of Europe. In the EEC the French had protected their own position with a series of safeguards, including a Common Agricultural Policy that was to work demonstrably in favour of France alone. The FRG, in spite of her increasingly greater economic weight, accepted this situation because Germans were anxious to underline their commitment to peace, reconciliation and liberal democracy. The basis of Britain's traditional policy of holding a balance of power in Europe had evaporated as a result of the war. France and Germany were no longer at loggerheads, and were united in their worries about the communist menace to the east. For the French, this menace should be met by a strong Europe standing independently from the United States and the Americans' British cat's-paw.

Germany might have been happier to accept both the Americans and the British, but the alliance with the French was even more important to them. Britain, as Dean Acheson put it, had lost an Empire and not found a new role.

In the wake of decolonization, Suez and the French veto, Britain had not looked so weak or forlorn for centuries. 'Never, surely,' wrote George Kennan, 'except under the impact of overwhelming military defeat . . . has a great country gone so rapidly from world power to extreme helplessness.' Yet, as David Reynolds commented, 'the tone of surprise is misplaced. Power is not a possession but a relationship.'[14] In one sense, Britain was beginning to pay the price for what had actually been a huge defeat in 1940, which had been interpreted as a victory. While Britain had chosen to remain unrealistically aloof from Europe, the legacy of 1940 had forged a new dynamic relationship between France and the FRG. Meanwhile, the frustrations of the pro-marketeers at de Gaulle's attitude were heightened by an increasingly well orchestrated campaign of anti-marketeering at home. Just as it was becoming clear that there was very little medium-term alternative to Europe economically, the anti-marketeers began to wake up a largely indifferent electorate with an increasingly jingoistic platform. The passing of de Gaulle from politics left the way clear for the most ardent Europhile in British politics, Edward Heath, to apply for a lucky third time. The negotiations were still tough: Britain's payments to Europe would be larger than most because of the taxing of her still considerable non-European trade. Much of this money would go to pay for the Common Agricultural Policy, which paid for 'inefficient' French agriculture. It was widely publicized that the cost of Britain's food bill might go up by as much as 25 per cent.

Supranationalism had meanwhile reared its ugly head again. At the Hague Summit of December 1969, where it had been agreed to consider Britain's new application, the Six had accepted that European co-operation should not only be widened but also deepened. There should be fuller co-operation in foreign affairs and a European Monetary Union was declared a long-term goal. Before Britain joined, Europe had agreed to a Common Fisheries Policy, though the details had not been worked out.[15] All these matters were to be deeply troubling to many people in Britain, who believed that the loss of freedom of action was too high a price to pay for economic co-operation. Hyperbole was becoming rife. The somewhat Euro-sceptical James Callaghan had already declared, somewhat elliptically, that the language of Chaucer was at stake. This was not, clearly, what Britain had fought in 1940 to preserve, only to concede in the peace.

There were signs that popular attitudes towards Europe were changing, though it is difficult to see that this translated itself into a political interest in the Community as such. In the 1960s and 1970s, the 'cultural revolution' that came with increased affluence, especially for the young, produced a more cosmopolitan outlook, reflected in one way in the huge increase in British holidays on the Continent. True, the EEC countries tended to be favoured only by the middle class, largely no doubt because they were much more expensive to visit than Spain, and the package holiday evolved in effect to insulate the average holidaying family from the local culture. Also, the fact that a foreign resort was so often 'full of Germans' spoiled many a British jingo's vacation. Elizabeth David began a revolution in British eating habits by the early 1960s, and Habitat championed a kind of Europeanism in its minimalist furniture design, as well as in introducing Britain to the garlic crusher.

Although such developments were initially limited to the professional middle class, they were elements in a recognizable growth of Francophilia in the 1960s and 1970s. Among the educated, this was further reflected in a new interest in French writer-philosophers such as Camus, Sartre and de Beauvoir. Between them, they educated the British in some of the moral and philosophical implications of living with defeat and occupation by the Nazis. Existentialism was 'cool' in the early 1960s, but the major developments in structuralism that were beginning to occur in French thinking in this period were to arrive in Britain via America, and rather later. On the whole, British philosophical thinking remained dominated by the empirical tradition of Bertrand Russell and A.J. Ayer. By and large, European thinking remained as alien as it had always been.

Postwar France and Italy went through a period of cultural adjustment much more radical than anything going on in postwar Britain, because those nations had to confront their pasts and define their futures in a much more serious way than a Britain relatively complacent in victory. Film was one obvious area where new radical approaches were developed. In neo-realism there developed a serious cinema culture, the impact of which did not really hit Britain until the end of the 1950s, and then only briefly. The comparatively stodgy British New Wave in film-making, confined to the narrow parameters of the realist tradition inherited from the documentary school, had petered out by the mid-1960s but aroused an interest in continental film-makers. Roman Polanski, Polish by birth but with strong French connections, made several seriously good films in Britain in this period, and the cult film-maker Michelangelo Antonioni made *Blow Up* in Britain in 1966.

Yet British cinema continued to be dominated by Hollywood even more than other national cinemas. The most significant film actor Britain produced in this period, Dirk Bogarde, did indeed turn to Europe rather than America, but he was the exception that proved the rule. Giving up the comfortable and easy career he had built for himself in Britain in the 1950s, he gained a new art-house audience in the 1960s working with the American émigré Joseph Losey, a political outsider who explored the social and sexual tensions of British society. By the late 1960s, Bogarde had despaired entirely of British cinema and turned instead to Luchino Visconti and Liliana Cavari to make films that centred on the sexual psychoses of Nazism, in *The Damned* and *The Night Porter*, and on homoeroticism, in *Death in Venice*. Making films that could not have been made in either Britain or America, he helped to raise the possibility of the development of a genuine pan-European cinema, centred on confronting the recent past. In Britain, however, these films confirmed Bogarde's reputation as a great actor but, even more, as an outsider.

The Swinging Sixties probably made Britain more interesting to continental Europeans than vice versa. The new cultural vibrancy in Britain seemed to suggest that Britain had emerged from its postwar stuffiness and become a more open, less class-ridden society, committed to modernization rather than preservation of the imperial ideals.[16] Yet there were elements of competition and opposition evident even here. The idea that London had suddenly overtaken Paris as the centre of the fashion industry was pooh-poohed by the French, who looked askance at the witty but somewhat tasteless statements made by the miniskirt and by Carnaby Street 'tat'. England's victory over West Germany in the World Cup seemed to footballers abroad to be a victory for a rather dour, mechanical style of play and had relied, anyway, on what many deemed a dubious goal.

Whatever the impact of these changes in culture, which involved at least an awareness and an acceptance of European chic, Europe as a political issue seems to have impinged on the consciousness of the British only when politicians decided to make it an issue. As places to visit, or as alternative cultures, mainland European countries may have become less alien, but voters seem to have been largely mystified by the significance of the EEC, with all its acronyms and its economic mechanisms.[17] The fact is that Europe has hardly been allowed at all to figure as a cultural or social issue in Britain, but only as a constitutional, political and economic one. European unity was an alien concept that had about it the faintest whiff of totalitarianism, another legacy of the European politics of the 1930s and the war years. It was an arrogance born of largely English ignorance of what living with land frontiers was really like. The Welsh and the Scots had understood this for hundreds of years however, and were soon to do something about it, as European integration undermined the rationale for a continued United Kingdom.

Not that the supposed special relationship with America had much more to recommend it than European unity. There was much resentment in Britain at the way the USA had taken over Britain's role as policeman of the world, and much resentment at the Americans' reluctance to share her nuclear secrets, even though the British had been involved in their initial uncovering. There was also widespread distaste at the continuing Americanization of British popular culture, even if the balance was temporarily corrected in the 1960s. The relationship had, anyway, always been more 'special' to the British than to the Americans. Churchill and Roosevelt had got along well personally, and the military men who had fought the war shoulder to shoulder developed a comradeship that was to last until that generation retired in the 1960s. Macmillan got on well with Kennedy, Callaghan with Carter, Thatcher with Reagan, Blair with Clinton. Deeper ties are harder to find, largely perhaps because there could be no question of an equal relationship.

Meanwhile, the Commonwealth also failed to provide a wholly attractive alternative. There was little in common between the member countries, other than that they had all been colonies of Britain. Canada, Australia and New Zealand naturally gravitated to the new Western superpower. Anti-marketeers referred to the loyalty of the Empire in 1940 as one reason for not letting down the Commonwealth in pursuit of the European chimera; but there were severe tensions. Apartheid in South Africa and white minority rule in Rhodesia-Zimbabwe kept alive the racist undertones of Empire that the idea of the Commonwealth was supposed to allay and transform. New Commonwealth immigration into Britain set up major racist currents in British society as well, first evident in the Notting Hill riots of 1957 and constantly resurfacing in minor but ugly instances of British fascism, as well as in the barely guarded statements of more mainstream politicians such as Enoch Powell.

Europe became the seismic issue in British politics when Harold Wilson decided to renegotiate the terms of British entry and to allow a national referendum on the result. Although Britain was to vote by a two-to-one majority in favour of the renegotiated terms, the cross-party alliances that were formed in the referendum campaign were of great significance in redefining the axes of British politics. What was at stake, opponents of Europe on the Left and on the Right could agree, was national sovereignty, parliamentary democracy, the Britons' ability to do things the ways they wanted – national identity, in fact. From the mid-1970s to the mid-1990s, there was virtually no other issue in British politics that mattered, not even the increasingly dangerous situation in Northern Ireland. It divided both major parties into bitterly opposed groups. Enoch Powell's suggestion that anti-European Tories vote Labour in 1974 may have been the reason why Heath narrowly lost that election. Almost the entire work of the Wilson governments of 1974 to 1976 was taken up with renegotiation and the referendum, leaving no time to deal with other pressing issues of economic reform.[18]

Callaghan's government of 1976 to 1979 faced the equally divisive issue of direct elections to a European Parliament. The problem was further complicated by the Lib–Lab Pact, which was the only way Callaghan was able to retain a parliamentary majority. The Pact dovetailed the European issue into far-reaching domestic constitutional matters, for the Liberals were in favour not only of direct election to the European Parliament, which according to anti-Europeans threatened the sovereignty of Westminster, but also of proportional representation as a system of voting both in Europe and at home. In the event, direct voting was agreed but proportional representation was not. When it came to the crunch in the first Euro-elections in 1979, the diminutive turn-out demonstrated the remarkable lack of interest on the part of the electorate. Severe damage had been done to Labour. Pro-Europeans grew tired of the strident anti-Europeanism of the Left. When the Left gained control of the Party after Callaghan's departure as leader, the 'Gang of Four' left to form an alliance with the Liberals that was to be deeply detrimental to Labour's electoral position through the 1980s and early 1990s.

Europe was just as divisive an issue for the Conservatives, and for the same reasons. The British institutions that had survived the test of 1940 must not be surrendered to a supranational authority just because other countries had failed that test. The move of the Conservative Party to the Right occurred not so much because of the European issue but because of the failure of Heath's domestic policy. Still, it just happened to be true that the monetarist Right was also mostly dubiously pro-European; their ideological outlook necessarily involved attacking protectionism, taxation, overspending and bureaucracy – all of which were associated with Brussels. If the renegotiation, the referendum and the European elections had taken up an inordinate amount of British political time in the mid and late 1970s, it had also confirmed the suspicions of the European Community that Britain was going to continue to be a difficult and often disruptive partner.

Withdrawal from Europe was now not a serious option for Britain, not only because of the referendum result but because no one could offer a credible alternative to arresting Britain's relative economic decline. When the European project had begun in the 1950s, Britain was the richest country in Europe. By the time she entered the EEC, along with Eire and Norway, she was the third poorest of the Nine. The Euro-sceptics' efforts were now concentrated on the strategy of continuing to attempt to reform Europe in Britain's image and of belligerently defending national interests where supranationalism was involved. The results were, more often than not, counter-productive. Margaret Thatcher's single-minded campaign to secure a refund of British payments to Europe effectively tied up major European business for nearly four years in the early 1980s. Her defenders saw the Iron Lady standing up for British interests, her detractors saw her losing all sense of proportion: true, Britain paid more than any other member except Germany, but the entire EEC budget was only about as much as one big-spending British ministry, and all member nations, including Britain, only contributed slightly more or less than 1 per cent of their national income. It was a Pyrrhic victory as well, the critics argued, since the European taxation on Britain's external trade was reduced but all members' VAT contributions were increased, at just the point when British trade was becoming thoroughly oriented towards the European VAT-taxed market.

If Thatcher helped Britain regain some prestige in the world with her charismatic belligerence, it was at the expense of the goodwill of many of Britain's supposed partners in Europe and, ultimately, at the expense of her own leadership of the Conservative Party. She accepted and pushed forward vigorously the idea of a single European market, which was in line with the Conservative domestic strategy of a return to free market economics. She also accepted the widening of membership to include Spain, Portugal, South-eastern and Eastern Europe, partly for the same reason but partly, too, because she believed it would weaken the supranational tendencies at the core of Europe, the Franco–German axis. In fact, the single European market actually needed a vast new bureaucracy in Brussels and a raft of legislation to make it possible, taking away national rights over customs duties, currency controls and replacing them with uniform controls over the community as a whole. The Thatcher government quickly accepted this surrender of national sovereignty in the Single European Act. Then, in the train of the Single European Act came the Delors Plan, reinstating the goal of an Economic Monetary Union as the coherent next step. In its train, too, came the Social Charter to protect the underprivileged from the socially adverse effects caused by the single market.

In a speech delivered in Bruges, Thatcher appealed to the same set of values that Churchill had put to the electorate in 1945. While Churchill had warned then that a victory for individual freedom must not be sacrificed to state collectivism, Thatcher now warned that her government had not rolled back the frontiers of the postwar state in Britain to see them reimposed by a European superstate. David Reynolds argues that the Thatcher project for Europe was doomed from the start, that her insistence on national sovereignty was unreal, as a signatory both to the Treaty of Rome and the Single European Act. For her supporters, it created the illusion that Britain could still act independently in the world, but the seepage of authority was inexorable.[20] Gaullism succeeded as a strategy for France because France was at the core of the entire European project. Thatcherism could not do the same for Britain because Britain was comparatively marginal in that project, and had marginalized herself further by constantly opting out of European decisions which were then made without her, but with which she was subsequently obliged to comply anyway.

France's relations with Germany remained the dynamic of Western European development, as they had since the end of the Second World War, in the bid to ensure that 1940 could not happen again. While the end of the threat from the Warsaw Pact in the early 1980s removed one unifying issue, the continued development of the German economy, and the reunification of Germany, only reinforced German as well as French determination to ensure that both countries were so bound together that friction would never be possible again. That was what the legacy of Nazism and of occupation had made central to the development of European politics. Britain, a nation that had remained undefeated in 1940, never fully understood the forces for European unity unleashed by the humiliation of France and the shame of Germany. To maintain a balance of power in Europe was not an option for Britain after 1940. A mirage of Britain's former economic and military power and a mirage of the former divisions on mainland Europe – the twin elements that had made that balance of power policy possible for so long – continued to mesmerize the national vision of the world.

British sceptics have never believed that France can control Germany through the EEC and have always feared the EEC would prove to be a new and more peaceful route to German domination of the Continent. Thatcher showed no sympathy at all for German reunification but, in a double defeat for her policy at the Strasbourg European Council in December 1989, not only was there widespread support for reunification but the French won an agreement to draw up a treaty for European monetary union. Nicholas Ridley incautiously told a journalist the following year that European monetary union would be the road by which Germany would be able to achieve what Hitler had never managed to do: to take over the whole of Europe. Although Ridley was forced to resign, Thatcher's clear reluctance to let him go and her determination to sink monetary union was the beginning of the end of her premiership. In November 1990, when he resigned from the Cabinet, the mild-mannered Sir Geoffrey Howe launched an uncharacteristically bitter attack on the Prime Minister's attitudes to Europe and on her conduct of European policy, in particular the ease with which she used the word 'no'.

Michael Heseltine, another strong Europeanist who had resigned earlier on a related issue, challenged her for the leadership. In the resultant contest, the comparatively unknown John Major emerged as the compromise candidate between the pro-Europeans and the Euro-sceptics. That was not to be the end of it. Britain crashed out of the Exchange Rate Mechanism. The European issue continued to dog the Conservative administration until the defeat in the 1997 election, and also thereafter in opposition. It was almost a mirror rerun of Labour's crisis between 1976 and the mid-1980s. By the end of the century, neither Conservative nor Labour were prepared to make unequivocal statements about Britain joining the European Monetary Union. A few were prepared to reject it outright, but they were marginalized by the majority who decided to wait and see, looking to keep their options open and to maintain the right to decide. This stance disguises the fact that, as has so often been the case in Britain's European policy since the 1950s, the decision is much more likely to depend on what happens in Europe rather than on what happens in Britain.

Britain came out of the Second World War believing that she was still a great power. Indeed, *de facto* she was – one of the Big Three – but the implication that that precluded her from involving herself too closely in Europe did not follow. During the war the Foreign Office had come to believe that a closer political involvement in Europe should be an important element in her policy to control Germany, but politicians were not prepared to stomach the supranational elements that mainland European countries sorted out for themselves in the Schuman Plan. For many years after the war, Europe's economic arrangements did not suit Britain, because she was still a major world trading power. As it became clear that the Americans were not prepared to see Britain as an equal partner, and as the links and particularly the trade with the Commonwealth declined, first Macmillan and then Wilson came to see the European Community as the only way out for Britain as a means of preventing further decline.

It is of course fair to say that all nations that committed themselves to the European Community were making up for national failure. This is as true, in different ways, of post-Dictator Spain, Portugal and Greece as it is of France, Germany and Britain. But what has bedevilled Britain in Europe uniquely has been the collective understanding that, for the British, membership has been a necessity rather than an ideal. This has been a particularly acute problem for the English, because if Europe threatened British national sovereignty, it also threatened England's hegemony in the United Kingdom as a result. Anthony Sampson asked in the 1970s what a working-class man in Dundee had in common with a working-class man in Manchester, except for the fact that they were both ruled by public schoolboys in London, an alien city for most of the Britons who did not live there.[21] The federal idea, and the Regional Fund, gave new confidence and new credibility to the Scottish National Party and Plaid Cymru, especially as Europe began to lose its cachet as a 'capitalist club' and adopted welfarist credentials. The Celtic nationalists within the United Kingdom could pledge the economic future of their nations to a larger, progressive Europe rather than to an Anglocentric, failing Britain.

Looked at in the context of the wider world since 1945, it is clear that, like it or not, the pressures of globalization would have forced Britain to concede some of her sovereignty. Every nation in the West has had to put up with the consequences for nationhood of multinational corporations and international banks, some of which have the economic clout of fairly sizeable countries. This has not been nearly as galling for the British as the loss of sovereignty to Europe. For Britain, membership was a signifier of her decline rather than of her rebirth, as it has been for France, Germany, Spain, Portugal and Ireland, and may prove to be for Scotland and Wales. As a result, Britain has obfuscated, delayed, opted out.

The offshore islanders of Europe, more isolated from European events than ever before by the experience of 1940, still find it difficult to come to terms with the fact that isolation is not always heroic or splendid, even if it may have been in 1940. After her resignation, Lady Thatcher smelled what she called 'appeasement' among those who would be prepared to sell Sterling to the Delors Plan and monetary union. In 1999, attending her first Conservative Party conference for nine years, she declared that in her lifetime all the problems had come from mainland Europe, and all the solutions had come from 'the English-speaking peoples'. That last, Churchillian phrase allowed many in her own party to dismiss her as outdated but, at the same conference, William Hague still found time to bracket Churchill and the British people in 1940 with Thatcher and Major and the British people in the 1990s, as examples of the great tradition of 'conservative forces' that Tony Blair had recently condemned. Tony Blair and the New Labour–New Britain project seem prepared at least to soften the rhetoric on Europe. By and large, however, it remains significantly true that when the German and French media use the term 'Europe', they mean 'us'; when the British media use the term, they mean 'them'.

9 Conclusion

The myths that I have been tracing have organized the preparation for, the experience and the aftermath of the most dangerous year in modern British history. These myths were not 'lies'. They are not to be judged for their truth-value, as such, but for what they tell us about the period in which they circulated, and how they were reworked in subsequent, and different, times. In the years between 1918 and 1939, Britain had been deeply worried by the prospect of another war, and understandably so. Air warfare threatened to impact on British society in a way that the Great War, by a small margin, had not quite done. Though Germany, Austria-Hungary and Russia had collapsed under the strain of total war, Britain had managed to adapt and survive and, although it soon hardly seemed worth the cost, to win. The impact of the depression of the interwar years, the central political issue for so long, served to confirm for the political elite that the future of advanced industrial, urbanized Britain was poised on something of a knife's edge. If the bombers ever came, and if they were always to get through, then the tensions that were only just being held in check by peacetime politics might well be unbearable, and Britain could go down the totalitarian path that was affecting so much of the contemporary European mainland. The threat of air power to the home country was compounded by the international threat to the Empire, on three widely separated fronts. The appeasers were faced with an unprecedentedly dangerous world, with the homeland apparently vulnerable as never before and the over-extended Empire also perilously exposed.

Chamberlain and his colleagues decided to concentrate on what they saw as the central threat, on which all other threats depended. If Germany, with her worryingly large and expanding air force, could be appeased, the threats from Italy and Japan could be dealt with piecemeal. This was a rational but still dangerous course to follow, for, if the appeasement of Germany failed, there would be nothing with which to fight. The great fear for the future may well have been the product of a depressed faith in democracy, a fear of the people in a revolutionary age, but at least it made the reality of the crisis in 1940 that much easier to bear. The fact that the strategic situation was even worse in 1940 than had been envisaged in turn provided the premise for the myth of the People's War, of the extraordinary resilience of the nation, and the people freed from the fearfulness and dubious politics of the Guilty Men.

The crisis itself, the need for maximum production and the destruction wrought by the Blitz, demanded explanations that both criticized the past and promised the future. The strategy of collectivism which began to emerge in 1940, and which took fuller shape in the ensuing years around the Beveridge Report, was to *assume* consensus. All right-thinking people, the collectivists suggested, already knew that things would have to change, and along particular lines which involved primacy for planning and for professional expertise in social matters, not the amateur haphazard methods of former times. Such was the lesson, and the opportunity, provided by the piecemeal emergency measures necessary to overcome what the Guilty Men had failed to do. There was little organized opposition to this story of how victory had been snatched from the jaws of defeat during the war. In assuming consensus, the collectivists had conjured that consensus into the centre of political common sense.

Churchill did not share such a view of the war. His war was for the survival of the Empire abroad and the British tradition of stout independence at home. His heroes were 'the few' who protected the many. The power of his rhetoric and his charismatic leadership provided an alternative self-image for Britain in the war, though it was temporarily overborne by the sentiments engendered by the collective effort, sentiments which were to find their symbol in the Beveridge Report. By the time of the 1945 General Election, a majority of British people was prepared to express their support for the politicians who had guided them on the home front since 1940. The real political shift had occurred in 1940, when an unprecedented crisis in British history had demanded extraordinary measures and extraordinary commitment. The rest of the war at home, once the immediate crisis was past, had been a campaign to carry through the implications of that crisis, or a campaign to try to limit those implications. Churchill, as warlord, had neither the time nor perhaps the energy to control the drift to the Left.

For Labour in the immediate postwar years, the spirit of 1940 was still needed to build the New Jerusalem. But by the beginning of the

1950s, Conservative forces had regrouped to tell their different story of 1940: that the war had been fought to free the British people, not to fetter them to a state machine, and that it was time the people enjoyed the fruits of that victory. The consumer economy that had already begun to make a measurable impact in the 1930s, the other side of 'the hungry Thirties', allowed Labour's welfare revolution to be maintained, if not expanded, but the inflationary pressures injected into the system by One Nation Toryism were soon to take their toll of the Keynes–Beveridge axis.

As public expenditure became a juggernaut in the 1960s and 1970s, and as it became clear that whatever else the war had done to Britain it had not halted her relative decline as a world trading power, Conservative monetarists decided on a campaign to 'free the people' once more. In this campaign the New Right was aided by a war in the South Atlantic which allowed them to re-focus the story of 1940, to retell it as a war against dictators for freedom – but this time wrenched free from the collectivist implications of a People's War. In the major realignment of the first half of the 1980s, the Left lost the moral high ground it had occupied in 1940, consolidated in 1945 and guarded, even in opposition, from the 1950s through to the 1970s.

In international affairs, this story was largely reversed. Britain assumed that standing alone against the dictator in 1940 had bequeathed her a loud voice in the postwar world, particularly in a Europe that had buckled so quickly under Hitler's pressure. There was little collectivism evident in Britain's international policy; rather there was the attempt to shore up her independence and sovereignty. It proved to be an illusion that the 'special relationship' with America would keep Britain afloat. Britain had been kept going by the Americans after her virtual bankruptcy in 1940 because it was in America's interest to prevent Britain from falling. It was unrealistic to believe that America would go on being thankful to Britain once the Nazi threat had passed and once another superpower had arisen to occupy the centre of America's international attention. It was an illusion, too, that a Commonwealth of former colonies would go on providing a platform for the erstwhile Imperial power. Just as illusory was the belief that Europe needed or even wanted British leadership, and when Britain finally entered the EEC it was because there appeared to be no alternative to prevent her continued decline. By the 1990s, Britain had surrendered to the inevitable collectivism of European affairs, but there were still to be major alarms and excursions over the details.

I have argued that myths are the big stories of history, that they frame the details of how we think about the past. Yet, when the context becomes too angular to fit cosily within the framework of the myth, the myth must adapt or give way. Until the 1980s, for example, historians described as a consensus that had emerged from wartime national unity what we would now see as quite distinctive interpretations of collectivism in the 1950s and 1960s. There were really no new facts about the postwar years to appear in the 1980s and 1990s to upset this earlier representation, but the context in which the wartime myth was encountered had certainly changed as the Keynes–Beveridge axis collapsed. This is why Thatcher had the opportunity she did, not because the newly dominant view of the past was innately more truthful than the one it succeeded.

In a period when the myths no longer carry their original ideological weight, we would still accept that 1940 was a victory of sorts. It was a victory for national institutions and for progressive social attitudes. But it was also a victory for traditional attitudes to the outside world, as well as for English self-belief as the nation at the core of the United Kingdom. We would still accept, too, that 1940 began a sort of revolution in social politics, but perhaps that would have happened anyway; the pre-1914 social legislation had expanded in the interwar years and the consumer economy was already making Britain a richer country before 1940. Anyway, the Beveridge assumptions of universality and comprehensiveness have hardly survived the Thatcher revolution, and Britain's social policies are no more progressive now than many European countries with very different experiences of the war. Britain struggled hard to transform her imperial past in the postwar years but looked to justify it, too, in a Commonwealth idea that had no realistic base in geopolitical or economic terms. In Europe, 1940 worked to proclaim Britain's superiority and her destiny to lead the Continent. As a result, European integration has probably been delayed; if not, there is one thing we would certainly accept: that it has not been shaped in the way Britain would have preferred and with which she can feel entirely happy. Britain has had to learn by a slower and more circuitous route than the rest of Europe that 'very well, alone!' can be a slogan only for unprecedented emergencies.

Notes

1 Introduction

1 C. Ponting, *1940: Myth and Reality*, Hamish Hamilton, London, 1990.
2 B. Anderson, *Imagined Communities: Reflections on the Origin and Spread of Nationalism*, Verso, London, 1991.
3 C. Lévi-Strauss, *Myth and Memory*, Routledge and Kegan Paul, London, 1978, p. 43,
4 See esp. P. Ransome, *Antonio Gramsci*, Harvester, Brighton, 1992.
5 See esp. P. Rabinow, *The Foucault Reader*, Penguin, Harmondsworth, 1991.
6 N.Z. Davies, *The Return of Martin Guerre*, Penguin, Harmondsworth, 1983.
7 R. Barthes, 'Introduction to the structural analysis of narratives', in S. Heath (ed.), *Image, Music, Text*, Fontana, London, 1977.
8 R. Rosenstone, *Visions of the Past: The Challenge of Film to our Idea of History*, Harvard University Press, Cambridge, MA, 1995; *Revisioning History: Film and the Construction of a New Past*, Princeton University Press, Princeton, NJ, 1995.
9 C.L. Mowat, *Britain Between the Wars*, Methuen, London, 1955, p. 657. See also J. Baxendale and C. Pawling, *Narrating the Thirties: A Decade in the Making: 1930 to the Present*, Macmillan, Basingstoke, 1996.
10 Mass Observation, *Peace and the Public*, Mass Observation Archive, p. 58.
11 A. Calder, *The People's War*, Cape, London, 1969.
12 T. Harrisson, *Living through the Blitz*, Collins, London, 1976.
13 C. Barnett, *The Audit of War: The Illusion and Reality of Britain as a Great Power*, Macmillan, London, 1986.
14 A. Calder, *The Myth of the Blitz*, Pimlico, London, 1992.
15 Calder, *Myth*, Ch. 5; N. Harman, *Dunkirk: The Necessary Myth*, Coronet, London, 1981.
16 Calder, *Myth*, p. 272.
17 Ibid., p. 195.
18 D. Reynolds, '1940: fulcrum of the twentieth century?', *International Affairs*, 66, 1990, pp. 325–50.

2　The projection of war, 1918 to 1939

1　Viscount Templewood (Sir Samuel Hoare), *Nine Troubled Years*, Collins, London, 1954, p. 394.
2　M. Cooper, *The Birth of Independent Air Power*, Allen & Unwin, London, 1986.
3　S. Baldwin, *House of Commons Debates*, 10 November 1932.
4　S. Baldwin, *House of Commons Debates*, 30 July 1934.
5　A.M. Low, *Modern Armaments*, Scientific Book Club, London, 1939, pp. 200–2.
6　See H. Moon, *The Invasion of the United Kingdom: Public Controversy and Official Planning*, unpublished Ph.D. thesis, University of London, 1968.
7　A. Eden, *Facing the Dictators*, Cassell, London, 1967, p. 18.
8　G. Douhet, *The Command of the Air* (trans. D. Ferrari), Collins, London, 1940.
9　See M. Smith, *British Air Strategy between the Wars*, Oxford University Press, Oxford, 1984, Ch. 3.
10　I.F. Clarke, *Voices Prophesying War*, Fontana, London, 1966, p. 164.
11　E. Shanks, *People of the Ruins; a Story of the English Revolution and After*, Stokes, New York, 1920.
12　'Miles' (Neil Bell), *The Gas War of 1940*, Scolartis, London, 1931.
13　G. Cornwallis-West, *The Women who Stopped War*, Hutchinson, London, 1935.
14　E. Linklater, *The Impregnable Women*, Jonathan Cape, London, 1938.
15　See P. Miles and M. Smith, *Cinema, Literature and Society*, Croom Helm, London, 1987, Part 1, Ch. 3.
16　G. Orwell, *Keep the Aspidistra Flying*, Gollancz, London, 1936, repr. Penguin, Harmondsworth, 1962 p. 21.
17　G. Orwell, *Homage to Catalonia*, Gollancz, London, 1938, repr. Penguin, 1980, p. 246. See Miles and Smith, *Cinema, Literature and Society*, Part 3, Ch. 2.
18　*All Quiet on the Western Front*, dir. L. Milestone, Universal, USA, 1930; *Wings*, dir. W. Wellman, Paramount, USA, 1927; *Hell's Angels*, dir. and prod. H. Hughes, USA, 1930. See M. Paris, *From the Wright Brothers to Top Gun: Aviation, Nationalism and Popular Cinema*, Manchester University Press, Manchester, 1995.
19　*Things to Come*, dir. W.C.Menzies, London Films, UK, 1936.
20　'Guernica', *Gaumont British News*, 6 May 1937, Visnews Archive.
21　'The Four Power Conference', *Gaumont British News*, 3 October 1938, reproduced on InterUniversity History Film Consortium videocassette, *Neville Chamberlain*. See also their videocassette on *Stanley Baldwin*.
22　Cabinet minutes, 24 September 1938, *Cab 23/95*.
23　'Estimated scale of attack from the air on England . . .', Home Defence Committee, June 1937, p. 2, *Cab 53/32*.
24　J.S. Meisel, 'Air raid shelter policy and its critics in Britain before the Second World War', *Twentieth Century British History*, Vol 5, No 1, 1994, pp. 300–19.
25　See J. Charmley, *Churchill, The End of Glory: A Political Biography*, Hodder & Stoughton, London, 1993.
26　G. Lansbury, *House of Commons Debates*, 3 September 1939.

3   To Dunkirk

1 C. Ponting, *1940: Myth and Reality*, Hamish Hamilton, London, 1990, p. 138.
2 Quoted in I. Mclaine, *Ministry of Morale: Home Front Morale and the Ministry of Information*, Allen & Unwin, London 1979, p. 27.
3 Ibid., p.39.
4 *The Times*, 23 September 1939.
5 T. Harrisson (ed.), *War Begins at Home*, Chatto & Windus, London, 1940.
6 Home Intelligence Daily Report, 5 August 1940, *INF 1/264*.
7 Home Intelligence Report, 8 May 1940, *INF 1/264*.
8 *Manchester Guardian*, 11 May 1940.
9 *Daily Express*, 24 May 1940.
10 *The Times*, 13 May 1940.
11 For a full account of the Battle of France, see B. Bond, *France and Belgium, 1939–1940*, Davis Poynter, London, 1975.
12 *Daily Express*, 31 May 1940.
13 N. Harman, *Dunkirk: The Necessary Myth*, Hodder & Stoughton, London, 1980, p. 243.
14 B. Stubbs, Commentary, Dover, *BBC Archives*, May 1940.
15 Meeting of the Supreme War Council, 11 June 1940, *CAB 99/3*.
16 See e.g. L. Lévy, *The Truth about France*, Penguin Special, London, 1941.
17 M. Muggeridge, *The Thirties: 1930–1940 in Britain*, Weidenfeld & Nicolson, 1940; R. Graves and A. Hodge, *The Long Weekend: A Social History of Great Britain, 1918–1939*, Faber and Faber, London, 1940.
18 Cato, *Guilty Men*, Gollancz, London, 1940, p.11.
19 Ibid., p. 43.
20 Ibid., p. 48.
21 Ibid., p. 63.
22 Ibid., p. 78.
23 Ibid., p. 125.
24 G. Orwell, 'My country right or left', *Collected Essays, Journalism and Letters, Vol 2*, Penguin, Harmondsworth, 1975.
25 J.B. Priestley, *Postscripts*, Heinemann, London, 1940, pp. 2–4.
26 Harman, *The Necessary Myth*, pp. 164–5.
27 A. Eden, *Tonight's Talk*, 26 June 1940, *BBC Archives*.
28 S. Nicholas, '"Sly demagogues" and wartime radio', in J.B. Priestley and the BBC, *Twentieth Century British History*, Vol 6, No 3, 1995, 247–66, p. 253.
29 Priestley, *Postscripts*, p. 12.
30 Ibid., p. 38.
31 Nicholas, '"Sly demagogues"' p. 262.
32 W.S. Churchill, *Into Battle*, Cassell, London, 1947, p. 251.
33 *Dawn Guard*, dir. R. and J. Boulting, Ministry of Information, 1940.
34 See e.g. S. Baldwin, *On England and Other Addresses*, Philip Allan, London, 1933.
35 Priestley, *Postscripts*, p. 100.

4   Invasion and the Battle of Britain

1 A.P. Herbert, *The Thames*, Weidenfeld & Nicholson, London, 1966, p. 160.
2 *Evening Standard*, 7 June 1940.
3 *Cab 24/287* CP 149 (39), 3 July 1939.
4 *Cab 66/7* WP 168 (40), 25 May 1940.
5 W. Churchill, *House of Commons Debates*, 4 June 1940.
6 WP (40) 324, *CAB 66/11*.
7 The discussions can be followed, though only rather opaquely, in *CAB 65/13*, Cabinet conclusions of 27 and 28 June and *CAB 65/7*, Cabinet conclusions of 19 and 24 July.
8 C. Ponting, *1940: Myth and Reality*, Hamish Hamilton, London, 1990, p. 118.
9 D. Reynolds, 'Churchill and the British Decision to fight on in 1940', in R. Langhorne (ed.), *Diplomacy and Intelligence during the Second World War*, Cambridge University Press, Cambridge, 1985.
10 *Statistical Digest of the War*, HMSO, London, 1951, p. 152.
11 See M. Smith, *British Air Strategy between the Wars*, Oxford University Press, Oxford, 1984.
12 A. Calder, *The People's War*, Jonathan Cape, London, 1969, p. 117.
13 E. Bevin, *The Job To Be Done*, W. Heinemann, London, 1942, p. 26.
14 G. Beckles, *Birth of a Spitfire*, Collins, London, 1941, pp. 109–20.
15 See T. Wintringham, *New Ways of War*, Penguin Special, London, 1940.
16 T. Wintringham, 'The Home Guard can fight', *Picture Post*, 21 September 1940.
17 C. Graves, *The Home Guard of Britain*, Hutchinson, London, 1943.
18 *Statistical Digest*, p. 8.
19 M. Jullian, *Battle of Britain*, Cape, London, 1967, p. 41.
20 J.R. Taylor, *A Dream of England*, Manchester University Press, Manchester, 1994.
21 *Radio Times*, 14 June 1940.
22 *The Times*, 1 July 1940.
23 I. Macleod, *Neville Chamberlain*, Muller, London, 1962.
24 Mass Observation report 496, *Popular Attitudes to Wartime Politics*, 20 November 1940.
25 A. Calder, *People's War*, p. 140.
26 L. Walmsley, *Fishermen at War*, Collins, London, 1941, p. 255.
27 *The Battle of Britain*, dir. G. Hamilton, UA/Spitfire, 1969.
28 For a fuller narrative of the Battle of Britain, see B. Collier, *The Defence of the United Kingdom*, HMSO, London, 1957; R. Wright, *Dowding and the Battle of Britain*, Penguin, London, 1969.
29 Compare cinematic treatment of the Battle with those of veterans of the Battle in P. Addison and J. Crang (eds), *The Burning Blue*, Pimlico, London, 2000.
30 *First of the Few*, dir. Leslie Howard, Melbourne/British Aviation films, GB, 1942.
31 H. Trevor Roper (ed.), *Hitler's War Directives*, Pan, London, 1966.
32 G. Wright, *The Ordeal of Total War*, New York, Harper Row, 1968; P. Calvocoressi, G. Wint and J. Pritchard, *Total War*, London, Penguin, 1989.

33 Trevor Roper (ed.), *Hitler's War Directives.*
34 See K. Maier, 'Luftwaffe preparations', in P. Addison and J. Crang, *The Burning Blue*, Pimlico, London, 2000.
35 See R. Cecil, *Hitler's Decision to Invade Russia*, Davis-Poynter, London, 1975.
36 T. Taylor, *The Breaking Wave*, Weidenfeld & Nicolson, London, 1967, p. 188.
37 Priestley, *Postscripts*, 28 July 1941, p. 42.

5 The Blitz

1 *Daily Herald*, 16 November 1940.
2 See I.L. Janis, *Air War and Emotional Stress: Psychological Studies of Bombing and Civilian Defence*, McGraw Hill, New York, 1967.
3 R.M. Titmuss, *Problems of Social Policy*, HMSO, London, 1950.
4 T. Harrisson and C. Madge, *War Begins at Home*, Chatto & Windus, London, 1940, pp. 296–309.
5 T.H. O'Brien, *Civil Defence*, HMSO, London, 1950, pp. 532–40.
6 See e.g. J. McNicol, 'The evacuation of schoolchildren', in H.L. Smith (ed.), *War and Social Change*, Manchester University Press, Manchester, 1986, pp. 3–31. McNicol's argument is not so much that evacuation did not register real problems, but that there was no consensus on what should be done about them. My point is that the size of the problem, and its registration as a problem, was as important as the failure to find an acceptable solution.
7 R. Padley and M. Cole (eds), *Evacuation Survey*, Routledge, London, 1940; National Federation of Women's Institutes, *Town Children through Country Eyes*, NFWI, Dorking, 1940; Harrisson and Madge, *War Begins at Home.*
8 Women's Group on Public Welfare, *Our Towns*, Oxford University Press, Oxford, 1942.
9 *Statistical Digest of the War*, HMSO, London, 1951, p. 51.
10 S.M. Ferguson and H. Fitzgerald, *Studies in the Social Services*, HMSO, London, 1954, p. 222.
11 Home Intelligence Daily Report, 16 July 1940, *INF 1/264.*
12 N. Farson, *Bombers Moon*, Gollancz, London, 1941, p. 69.
13 H. Nicolson, *Diaries and Letters*, Vol 11, Atheneum, New York, 1967, p. 114.
14 *Manchester Guardian*, 16 September 1940.
15 *The Times*, 25 October 1940.
16 *The Times*, 27 December 1940.
17 T.H. O'Brien, *Civil Defence*, HMSO, London, 1957, p. 392.
18 R. Calder, *Carry On London*, English Universities Press, London, 1941, pp. 36–43.
19 F.R. Lewey, *Cockney Campaign*, Stanley Paul, London, 1944, p. 61.
20 F. Faviell, *A Chelsea Concerto*, Cassell, London, 1959, p. 118.
21 *Picture Post*, 4 January 1941.
22 *Fires Were Started*, dir. H. Jennings, Crown Film Unit, 1942.
23 A.P. Herbert, *The Thames*, Weidenfeld & Nicholson, London, p. 165.
24 Commentary by Tom Chalmers, 7 September 1940, *BBC Archives.*
25 *Daily Mail*, 31 December 1940.

26 *London Can Take It*, dir. H. Watt and H. Jennings, Crown Film Unit, 1940.
27 Report on Coventry, 18 November 1940, *Mass Observation Archive*.
28 *Daily Herald*, 16 November 1940.
29 *Manchester Guardian*, 16 November 1940.
30 *The Evening News*, 6 December 1940.
31 T. Harrisson, *Living Through the Blitz*, Collins, London, 1976.
32 Preparation of Air Raid Commentaries, 31 March 1941, *INF 1/174A*.
33 T. Harrisson (ed.), *War Begins at Home*, Chatto & Windus, London, 1940.
34 I. Mclaine, *Ministry of Morale: Home Front Morale and the Ministry of Information in World War 2*, Allen & Unwin, London, 1979, p. 87.
35 Ibid., p. 118.
36 Ibid., p. 136.
37 R. Titmuss, *Problems of the Social Services*, HMSO, London, 1957, p. 295; C.M. Kohan, *Works and Buildings*, HMSO, London, 1952, pp. 210–17.
38 T. Robbins, *Skinny Legs and All*, Bantam, New York, 1990, p. 142.
39 Harrisson, *Living Through the Blitz*, p. 188.
40 Very Revd R.T. Howard, 14–15 November 1940, *BBC Archives*.
41 A.T. Harris, *Bomber Offensive*, Collins, London, 1947.

6   Wartime politics and popular culture

1 Gallup International Opinion Polls, *Great Britain 1937–1975*, Random House, New York, 1976.
2 L. Noakes, *War and the British*, Taurus, London, 1977.
3 W.S. Churchill, *The Second World War* (abridged by D. Kelly), Penguin, Harmondsworth, 1969, p. 227.
4 Ibid., p. 361.
5 Ibid., p. 102.
6 Ibid., p. 228.
7 Ibid., p. 234.
8 Ibid., p. 357.
9 Ibid., pp. 359–60.
10 Ibid., p. 365.
11 G. Orwell, 'My country right or left', *Collected Essays, Journalism and Letters*, Vol 1, Penguin, Harmondsworth, 1975, p. 591.
12 G. Orwell, 'The English people', *CEJL*, Vol 3, p. 15.
13 G. Orwell, London Letter, Partisan Review, 1941, *CEJL*, Vol 2, p. 136.
14 *Picture Post*, 4 January 1941, p. 4.
15 Ibid.
16 Ibid., p. 9.
17 B.L. Coombes, *These Poor Hands*, Gollancz, London, 1939.
18 *Picture Post*, p. 17.
19 *Love on the Dole*, British National Films, London, dir. J. Baxter, 1941.
20 *Wales, Green Mountain, Black Mountain*, Crown Film Unit, dir. J. Eldridge, 1942.
21 *Diary for Timothy*, Crown Film Unit, dir. H. Jennings, 1945.
22 R.H. Titmuss, *Problems of Social Policy*, HMSO, London, 1957.
23 R.S. Sayers, *Financial Policy*, HMSO Longmans, London, 1956.

24 K. Jefferys, *The Churchill Coalition and Wartime Politics, 1940–1945*, Manchester University Press, Manchester, 1991; P. Addison, *The Road to 1945*, Cape, London, 1975.
25 See J. Harris, *William Beveridge*, Clarendon Press, Oxford, 1977; 'Some aspects of social policy in Britain during the Second World War', in W.J. Mommsen (ed.), *The Emergence of the Welfare State in Britain and Germany*, Croom Helm, London, 1981.
26 British Institute of Public Opinion, *The Beveridge Report and the Public*, BIPO, London, 1943, p. 14.
27 *Daily Mirror*, 2 December 1942, *New Statesman*, 27 March 1943.
28 *Daily Telegraph*, 2 December 1942.
29 Quoted in Jefferys, *The Churchill Coalition*, p. 237.
30 Jefferys, *The Churchill Coalition*, Ch. 5.
31 *Mr Churchill's Declaration of Policy to the Electors*, Conservative Party Central Office, 1945.
32 *Let Us Face the Future*, Labour Party, 1945.

7 Refighting the war: Attlee to Blair

1 P. Addison, *The Road to 1945*, Cape, London, 1975.
2 *Let Us Face the Future*, Labour Party, 1945.
3 *Mr Churchill's Declaration of Policy to the Electors*, Conservative Central Office, 1945.
4 See M. Smith, in B. Brivati and H. Jones (eds), *What Difference did the War Make?*, Leicester University Press, Leicester, 1993, pp. 35–48.
5 Labour Party, *Election Manifesto*, 1951.
6 See H.G. Nicholas, *The British General Election of 1950*, Macmillan, London, 1951.
7 See H. Macmillan, *Winds of Change*, Macmillan, London, 1966, pp. 1–3.
8 R. Hoggart, *The Uses of Literacy*, Chatto & Windus, London, 1957.
9 *Went the Day Well?*, dir. A. Cavalcanti, Ealing Films, 1942; C. Barr, *Ealing Studios*, Studio Vista, London, 1993, pp. 31–3.
10 *Passport to Pimlico*, dir. H. Cornelius, Ealing Films, 1949; J. Ellis, 'Made in Ealing', *Screen*, Vol 16. No 1, spring 1975, pp. 78–127.
11 *The Battle of Britain*, dir. G. Hamilton, UA/Spitfire, 1969.
12 A. Calder, *The People's War*, Jonathan Cape, London, 1969, p. 584.
13 L. Noakes, *War and the British*, Taurus, London, 1997.
14 *Sun*, 26 May 1982.
15 Jay, quoted in A. Busby, *Iron Britannia*, Allison & Busby, London, 1982, pp. 20–42.
16 J. Stevenson and C. Cook, *The Slump: Society and Politics During the Depression*, Cape, London, 1977.
17 *Guardian*, 1 October 1999.
18 *Guardian*, 8 October 1999.

8 America, Europe and the world

1 Gallup Report, *Attitudes to European Countries*, August 1983.
2 *Sunday Telegraph*, 28 August 1983.

3 M. Smith, *Democracy in a Depression*, University of Wales Press, Cardiff, 1998, p. 20.
4 P.J.V. Rollo, *Britain and the Briand Plan*, Keele University Press, Keele, 1972.
5 Memorandum by Orme Sargent, 'Stocktaking after VE Day', in R. Butler and M.E. Pelly (eds), *Documents on British Policy Overseas*, Series 1, Vol 1, HMSO, London, 1984, Document 102.
6 M.J. Hogan, *The Marshall Plan: America, Britain and the Reconstruction of Western Europe, 1947–1952*, Cambridge University Press, Cambridge, 1987, pp. 48–51; see also A. Milward, *The Reconstruction of Western Europe*, University of California Press, Berkeley, 1984.
7 A. Shlaim, *Britain and the Origins of European Unity, 1940–1951*, University of Reading, Reading, 1978; J.W. Young, *Britain, France and the Unity of Europe, 1945–1951*, Leicester University Press, Leicester, 1984.
8 See S. Dockrill, *Britain's Policy for West German Rearmament, 1950–55*, Cambridge University Press, Cambridge, 1991.
9 D. Reynolds, *Britannia Overruled: British Policy and World Power in the Twentieth Century*, Longman, London, 1991, p. 299.
10 T. Prittie, *Konrad Adenauer*, T. Stacey, London, 1972, p. 263.
11 R.J. Lieber, *British Politics and European Unity: Parties, Elites and Pressure Groups*, University of California Press, Berkeley, 1970, p. 207.
12 See N. Beloff, *The General Says No: Britain's Exclusion from Europe*, Penguin, Harmondsworth, 1963.
13 See U. Kitzinger, *The Second Try: Labour and the EEC*, Pergamon, Oxford, 1968.
14 Reynolds, *Britannia Overruled*, p. 293.
15 S. Young, *Terms of Entry: Britain's Negotiations with the EEC, 1970–1972*, Heinemann, London, 1973.
16 See A. Marwick, *The Sixties*, Oxford University Press, Oxford, 1998.
17 See R. Jowell and G. Hoinville (eds), *Britain into Europe; Public Opinion and the EEC, 1961–1975*, Croom Helm, London, 1976.
18 L.J. Robins, *The Reluctant Party: Labour and the EEC, 1961–1975*, Hesketh, Ormskirk, 1979.
19 See A.M. El-Agraa, *Britain Within the European Community*, Macmillan, London, 1983; see also P. Cosgrave, *Thatcher: The First Term*, Bodley Head, London 1985; S.R. Lewin, *The Anatomy of Thatcherism*, Fontana, London, 1992; J. Lodge (ed.), *The European Community and the Challenge of the Future*, Pinter, London, 1989; P. Ridell, *The Thatcher Government*, M. Robertson, Oxford, 1983; H. Young, *One of Us: A Biography of Margaret Thatcher*, Pan Macmillan, London, 1990.
20 D. Reynolds, *Britannia Overruled*. Longman, London, 1991.
21 A. Sampson, *A New Anatomy of Britain*, Stein & Day, New York, 1971.

Bibliography

Adamthwaite, A., *The Making of the Second World War*, Allen & Unwin, London, 1977.

Addison, P., *The Road to 1945*, Jonathan Cape, London, 1975.

Addison, P. and Crang, J. (eds), *The Burning Blue*, Pimlico, London, 2000.

Adelman, P., *British Politics in the 1930s and 1940s*, Cambridge University Press, Cambridge, 1997.

Agar, A., *Britain Alone, June 1940–June 1941*, Bodley Head, London, 1972.

Aldcroft, D.H., *The British Economy, 1920–1951*, Harvester, Brighton, 1986.

Aldgate, A. and Richards, J., *Britain Can Take It*, Blackwell, Oxford, 1986.

Alt, J.E., *The Politics of Economic Decline*, Cambridge University Press, Cambridge, 1979.

Anderson, B., *Imagined Communities*, Verso, London, 1991.

Ashford, D.E., *The Emergence of the Welfare State*, Blackwell, Oxford, 1986.

Balchin, N., *Darkness Falls from the Air*, Four Square, London, 1961.

Balcon, M., *A Lifetime of Films*, Hutchinson, London, 1969.

Baldwin, S., *On England and Other Addresses*, Philip Allan, London, 1933.

Balfour, M., *Propaganda in War, 1939–45*, Routledge & Kegan Paul, London, 1979.

Ball, S., *The Conservative Party and British Politics*, Longman, London, 1995.

Barker, E., *Britain in a Divided Europe*, Weidenfeld & Nicolson, London, 1971.

Barnett House Study Group, *London Children in Wartime Oxford*, Oxford University Press, Oxford, 1947.

Barnett, A., *Iron Britannia*, Allison & Busby, London, 1982.

Barnett, C., *The Audit of War*, Macmillan, London, 1986.

Barr, C. (ed.), *All Our Yesterdays: 90 Years of British Films*, BFI, London, 1986.

Barr, C., *Ealing Studios*, Studio Vista, London, 1993.

Bartlett, C.J., The *Long Retreat*, Macmillan, London, 1972.

Bartlett, C.J., *A History of Post-War Britain*, Bodley Head, Oxford, 1978.

Bartlett, V., *And Now Tomorrow*, Chatto & Windus, London, 1960.

Baxendale, J. and Pawling, C., *Narrating the Thirties*, Macmillan, Basingstoke, 1996.

Baylis, J., *Anglo–American Defence Relations*, Macmillan, London, 1981.

Bean, J.M.W. (ed.), *The Political Culture of Modern Britain*, Hamish Hamilton, London, 1987.

Beardmore, G., *Civilians at War: Journals, 1938–46*, Oxford University Press, Oxford, 1986.

Beckles, G., *Birth of a Spitfire*, Collins, London, 1941.

Beloff, N., *The General Says No*, Penguin, Harmondsworth, 1963.

Berlin, I., *Mr. Churchill in 1940*, Murray, London, 1964.

Berwick Sayers, W. (ed.), *Croydon and the Second World War*, Croydon Corporation, 1949.

Beveridge, W., *Social Insurance and Allied Services*, HMSO, London, 1942.

Bevin, E., *The Job To Be Done*, Heinemann, London, 1942.

Bialer, U., *The Shadow of the Bomber*, RHS, London, 1980.

Bisset, I., *The George Cross*, MacGibbon & Kee, London, 1961.

Blackaby, F.T. (ed), *British Economic Policy, 1960–1974*, Cambridge University Press, Cambridge, 1978.

Blackaby, F.T., *British Economic Management, 1960–1974*, Cambridge University Press, Cambridge, 1979.

Blake, J.W., *Northern Ireland in the Second World War*, HMSO, Belfast, 1956.

Blake, R., *The Conservative Party from Peel to Churchill*, Eyre & Spottiswoode, London, 1970.

Bogdanor, V., *Devolution*, CSC, London, 1979.

Bond, B., *France and Belgium, 1939–1940*, Davis Poynter, London, 1975.

Bond, B., *British Military Policy Between the Wars*, Oxford University Press, Oxford, 1980.

Boorman, J., *Hope and Glory*, Faber, London, 1987.

Brandon, H., *In the Red: The Struggle of Sterling, 1964–1966*, Deutsch, London, 1966.

Branson, N. and Heinemann, M., *Britain in the 1930s*, Weidenfeld & Nicolson, 1971.

Braybon, G. and Summerfield, P., *Out of the Cage*, Pandora, London, 1987.

Briggs, A., *History of Broadcasting in the UK, Vol. 3, The War of Words*, Oxford University Press, Oxford, 1970.

Briggs, S., *Keep Smiling Through*, Fontana, London, 1976.

British Institute of Public Opinion, *The Beveridge Report and the Public*, BIPO, London, 1943.

Brittain, V., *England's Hour*, Macmillan, London, 1941.

Brivati, B. and Jones, H. (eds), *What Difference did the War Make?*, Leicester University Press, Leicester, 1993.

Brockway, F., *Bermondsey Story*, Allen & Unwin, London, 1949.

Brooke, S., *Labour's War*, Oxford University Press, Oxford, 1992.

Brown, J., *The Heart of England*, Batsford, London, 1935.

Bruce-Gardyne, J., *Mrs Thatcher's First Administration*, Macmillan, London, 1984.

Bullock, A., *The Life and Times of Ernest Bevin*, 3 vols, Heinemann, London, 1960–84.

Butler, D., *The 1975 Referendum*, Macmillan, London, 1976.

Butler, D. (ed.), *Coalitions in British Politics*, Macmillan, London, 1978.

Butler, D. and Butler, G., *British Politics Facts, 1900–1985*, Macmillan, London, 1986.

Butler, D. and Stokes, D., *Political Change in Britain*, Macmillan, London, 1969.

Byrd, P. (ed.), *British Foreign Policy under Thatcher*, St Martins, London, 1988.

Calder, A., *The People's War*, Cape, London, 1969.

Calder, A., *The Myth of the Blitz*, Pimlico, London, 1992.

Calder, A. and Sheridan, D. (eds), *Speak for Yourself*, Oxford University Press, Oxford, 1985.

Calder, R., *Carry On London*, English Universities Press, London, 1941.

Calder, R., *Lesson of London*, Secker & Warburg, London, 1941.

Calvocoressi, P., Wint, G. and Pritchard, J., *Total War*, London, Penguin, 1989.

Cantril, H. (ed.), *Public Opinion 1935–46*, Princeton University Press, Cambridge MA, 1951.

'Cato', *Guilty Men*, Gollancz, London, 1940.

Ceadel, M., *Pacifism in Britain, 1914–45*, Oxford University Press, Oxford, 1980.

Cecil, R., *Hitler's Decision to Invade Russia*, Davis-Poynter, London, 1975.

Central Statistical Office, *Statistical Digest of the War*, HMSO, 1951.

Chapman, J., *The British at War*, Taurus, London, 1998.

Charmley, J., *Churchill, The End of Glory*, Hodder & Stoughton, London, 1993.

Chester, D. (ed.), *Lessons of the British War Economy*, Cambridge University Press, Cambridge, 1951.

Churchill, W.S., *Into Battle*, Cassell, London, 1947.

Churchill, W.S., *War Speeches*, Vol 1, Cassell, London, 1951.

Churchill, W.S., *The Second World War*, 6 vols, Cassell, London, 1948–54.

Churchill, W.S., *The Second World War* (abridged), Penguin, Harmondsworth, 1969.

Clark, F. Le Gros and Toms, R.W., *Evacuation – Failure or Reform*, Fabian Tract, London, 1940.

Clark, R.W., *Battle for Britain*, Harrap, London, 1965.

Clarke, I.F., *Voices Prophesying War*, Fontana, London, 1966.

Clarke, R., *Anglo–American Economic Collaboration in War and Peace*, Oxford University Press, Oxford, 1982.

Cole, J.A., *Lord Haw Haw*, Faber, London, 1964.

Collier, B., *The Defence of the United Kingdom*, HMSO, London, 1957.

Collier, B., *A Short History of the Second World War*, Collins, London, 1967.

Collier, R., *The City that Wouldn't Die*, Collins, London, 1959.

Colville, J., *The Fringes of Power: Downing Street Diaries*, 2 vols, Sceptre, London, 1986.

Coombes, B.L., *These Poor Hands*, Gollancz, London, 1939.

Cooper, M., *The Birth of Independent Air Power*, Allen & Unwin, London, 1986.

Cornwallis-West, G., *The Women who Stopped War*, Hutchinson, London, 1935.

Cosgrave, P., *Thatcher: The First Term*, The Bodley Head, London, 1985.

Crompton, R., *William and the Evacuees*, Newnes, London, 1940.

Cronin, J.E., *Labour and Society in Britain*, Batsford, London, 1984.

Crosby, T., *Civilian Evacuation in the Second World War*, Croom Helm, London, 1986.

Crosland, A., *The Future of Socialism*, Pickering, London, 1956.

Crosland, A., *Socialism Now*, Cape, London, 1974.

Cross, C., *The Fascists in Britain*, Barrie & Lockwood, London, 1961.

Crossman, R., *Planning for Freedom*, Hamish Hamilton, London, 1965.

Cudlipp, H., *Publish and Be Damned*, Dakers, London, 1953.

Darwin, B., *War on the Line*, Southern Railways, 1946.

Darwin, J., *Britain and Decolonisation*, St Martins Press, London, 1988.

Davies, N.Z., *The Return of Martin Guerre*, Penguin, Harmondsworth, 1983.

Delmer, S., *Black Boomerang*, Secker & Warburg, London, 1962.

Dockrill, S., *Britain's Policy for West German Rearmament, 1950–55*, Cambridge University Press, Cambridge, 1991.

Douhet, G., *The Command of the Air*, trans. D. Ferrari, Faber and Faber, London 1940.

Edelman, M., *Production for Victory, Not Profit!*, Gollancz, London, 1941.

Eden, A., *Facing the Dictators*, Cassell, London, 1967.

El-Agraa, A.M., *Britain Within the European Community*, Macmillan, London, 1983.

Ellis, J., 'Made in Ealing', *Screen*, Vol 16. No 1, spring 1975, pp. 78–127.

Fairfax, E., *Calling all Arms*, Hutchinson, London, 1945.

Farer, D., *The Sky's the Limit*, Hutchinson, London, 1943.

Farson, N., *Bombers Moon*, Gollancz, London, 1941.

Faviell, F., *A Chelsea Concerto*, Cassell, London, 1959.

Ferguson, S.M. and Fitzgerald, H., *Studies in the Social Services*, HMSO, London, 1954.

Finney, P. (ed.), *The Origins of the Second World War*, Arnold, London, 1997.

Firebrace, Sir A., *Fire Service Memories*, Melrose, London, 1949.

Fitzgibbon, C., *The Blitz*, Wingate, London, 1957.

Fleming, P., *Invasion 1940*, Hart Davis, London, 1957.

Foot, M., *Aneurin Bevan*, Vol 1, MacGibbon & Kee, London, 1962.

Fraser, D., *The Evolution of the Welfare State*, Macmillan, London, 1973.

Freedman, L., *Britain and Nuclear Weapons*, Macmillan, London, 1980.

Fussell, P., *Wartime*, Oxford University Press, New York, 1989.

Gallup Polls, *Great Britain 1937–75*, Random House, New York, 1976.

Gallup Report, *Attitudes to European Countries*, August 1983.

Gamble, A., *The Conservative Nation*, Routledge & Kegan Paul, London, 1974.

Gamble, A., *The Free Economy and the Strong State*, Macmillan, Basingstoke, 1988.

Gledhill, C. and Swanson, J., *Nationalising Femininity*, Manchester University Press, Manchester, 1996.

Gollancz, V. (ed.), *The Betrayal of the Left*, Gollancz, London, 1941.

Gorham, M., *Broadcasting and Television since 1900*, Dakers, London, 1952.

Gosden, P., *Education in the Second World War*, Methuen, London, 1976.

Grafton, P., *You, You and You: The People Out of Step*, Pluto, London, 1981.

Graham, P. and Graham, L., *Collar the Lot!*, Quartet, London, 1980.

Grant, I. and Marren, N., *The Countryside at War*, Jupiter, London, 1976.

Graves, C., *The Home Guard of Britain*, Hutchinson, London, 1943.

Graves, C., *London Transport Carried On*, London Transport, London, 1947.

Graves, R. and Hodge, A., *The Long Weekend*, Faber and Faber, London, 1940.

Guedella, P., *Mr. Churchill: A Portrait*, Hodder & Stoughton, London, 1941.

Halsey, A.H., *British Social Trends Since 1900*, Macmillan, Basingstoke, 1988.

Hampstead Borough Council, *Hampstead at War*, 1947.

Hancock, K. and Gowing, M., *British War Economy*, HMSO, London, 1953.

Harman, N., *Dunkirk: The Necessary Myth*, Coronet, London, 1981.

Harris, A.T., *Bomber Offensive*, Collins, London, 1947.

Harris, Sir A., *Bomber Offensive*, Collins, London, 1947.

Harris. J., *William Beveridge*, Clarendon Press, Oxford, 1977.

Harrisson, T., 'What is public opinion?', *Political Quartlery*, Vol x1, No 4, 1940.

Harrisson, T., 'Public opinion about Russia', *Political Quarterly*, Vol 12, No 4, 1941, pp. 353–66.

Harrisson, T., *War Factory*, Gollancz, London, 1943.

Harrisson, T., *Living Through the Blitz*, Collins, London, 1976.

Harrisson, T. and Madge, C., *War begins at Home*, Chatto & Windus, London, 1940.

Harrod, R., *The Prof*, Macmillan, London, 1959.

Harvie, C., *Scotland and Nationalism*, Allen & Unwin, London, 1977.

Harvie, C., *No Gods and Precious Few Heroes, Scotland, 1914–80*, Arnold, London, 1981.

Heath, S. (ed.), *Image, Music, Text*, Fontana, London, 1977.

Henderson, N., *The Birth of NATO*, Weidenfeld & Nicolson, London, 1982.

Hennessy, P., *Never Again: Britain 1945–51*, Vintage, London, 1993.

Henrey, R., *The Siege of London*, Dent, London, 1946.

Herbert, A.P., *The Thames*, Weidenfeld & Nicolson, London, 1966, p. 160.

Hillary, R., *The Last Enemy*, Macmillan, London, 1942.

HMSO, *Front Line: The Official Story of the Civil Defence of Britain*, HMSO, London, 1942.

HMSO, *Persuading the People*, HMSO, London, 1995.

HMSO, *Statistical Digest of the War*, HMSO, London, 1951.

Hodgkinson, A.W. and Sheratsky, E., *Humphrey Jennings*, University Press of New England, 1982.

Hodgson, V., *Few Eggs and No Oranges*, Dennis Dobson, London, 1976.

Hodson, J.L., *Through the Dark Night*, Gollancz, London, 1941.

Hodson, J.L., *Towards the Morning*, Gollancz, London, 1941.

Hogan, M.J., *The Marshall Plan*, Cambridge University Press, Cambridge, 1987.

Hoggart, R., *The Uses of Literacy*, Chatto & Windus, London, 1957.

Hornby, W., *Factories and Plant*, HMSO, London, 1958.

Hurstfield, J., *The Control of Raw Materials*, HMSO, London, 1953.

Hynes, S., *The Auden Generation*, The Bodley Head, Oxford, 1976.

Idle, E., *War over West Ham*, Faber, London, 1943.

Ingersoll, R., *Report on England*, The Bodley Head, Oxford, 1941.

Ingles, G.H., *When the War Came to Leicester*, C. Brooks, Leicester, 1945.

Inglis, R., *The Children's War*, Collins, London, 1989.

Inman, P., *Labour in the Munitions Industry*, HMSO 1957.

Isaacs, S. (ed.), *The Cambridge Evacuation Survey*, Methuen, London, 1941.

Janis, I.L., *Air War and Emotional Stress*, McGraw Hill, New York, 1951.

Jay, D., *After the Common Market*, Penguin, Harmondsworth, 1968.

Jefferys, K., *The Churchill Coalition and Wartime Politics*, Manchester University Press, Manchester, 1991.

Jeffrey, I., *The British Landscape, 1920–50*, Thames & Hudson, London, 1984.

Johnson, B.S., *The Evacuees*, Gollancz, London, 1968.

Jowell, R. and Hoinville, G. (eds), *Britain into Europe*, Croom Helm, London, 1976.

Jullian, M., *Battle of Britain*, Cape, London, 1967.

Kavanagh, D., *Thatcherism and British Politics*, Clarendon, Oxford, 1987.

Kavanagh, T., *Tommy Handley*, Hodder & Stoughton, London, 1949.

Kavanagh, D. and Morris, P., *Consensus Politics*, Oxford University Press, Oxford, 1989.

Kee, R., The *World We Left Behind*, Weidenfeld & Nicolson, London, 1984.

Kentish, L.W., *Home Guard – Bux4*, Lock, London, 1946.

Kirkham, P. and Thoms, D. (eds), *War Culture*, Lawrence & Wishart, London, 1995.

Kitzinger, U., *The Second Try: Labour and the EEC*, Pergamon Press, Oxford, 1968.

Klein, H., *The Second World War in Fiction*, Macmillan, Basingstoke, 1984.

Knowles, B., *Southampton – The English Gateway*, Hutchinson, London, 1951.

Kohan, C.H., *Works and Buildings*, HMSO, London, 1952.

Kops, B., *The World is a Wedding*, MacGibbon & Kee, London, 1963.

Lafitte, F., *The Internment of Aliens*, Penguin, London, 1940.

Lancum, F.H., *Press Officer – Please!*, Crosby Lockwood, London, 1946.

Langhorne, R. (ed.), *Diplomacy and Intelligence During the Second World War*, Cambridge University Press, Cambridge, 1985.

Laybourn, K., *The Evolution of British Social Policy*, Keele University Press, Keele, 1995.

Lent, A., *Blackout*, Princeton University Press, Princeton, NJ, 1991.

Lévi-Strauss, C., *Myth and Meaning*, Routledge & Kegan Paul, London, 1978.

Lévy, L., *The Truth about France*, Penguin Special, London, 1941.

Lewey, F.R., *Cockney Campaign*, Stanley Paul, London, 1944.

Lewin, S.R., *The Anatomy of Thatcherism*, Fontana, London, 1992.

Lewis, J., *Women in Britain since 1945*, Blackwell, Oxford, 1992.

Lewis, P., *A People's War*, Methuen, London, 1986.

Lieber, R.J., *British Politics and European Unity*, University of California Press, Berkeley, 1970.

Linklater, E., *The Impregnable Women*, Jonathan Cape, London, 1938.

Liverpool Daily Post and Echo, Bombers over Merseyside, 1943.

Lodge, J. (ed.), *The European Community and the Future*, Pinter, London, 1989.

Low, A.M., *Modern Armaments*, Scientific Book Club, London, 1939.

Lowe, R., *Education and the Second World War*, Falmer Press, London, 1992.

McCallum, R. and Readman, A., *The British General Election of 1945*, Oxford University Press, Oxford, 1947.

Mackay, R., *The Test of War, Inside Britain, 1939–45*, UCL Press, London, 1999.

McKee, A., *Strike from the Sky*, Souvenir Press, London, 1960.

Mackenzie, J., *Propaganda and Empire*, Manchester University Press, Manchester, 1984.

Mclaine, I., *Ministry of Morale*, Allen & Unwin, London, 1979.

Macleod, I., *Neville Chamberlain*, Muller, London, 1962.

Macmillan, H., *Winds of Change*, Macmillan, London, 1966.

Madge, C. and Harrisson, T., *Britain by Mass Observation*, Penguin Special, London, 1939.

Marchant, H., *Women and Children Last*, Gollancz, London, 1941.

Martin, K., 'Public opinion during the first six months', *Political Quarterly*, Vol x1, 1940.

Marwick, A., *Britain in the Century of Total War*, Penguin, London, 1970.

Marwick, A., *The Sixties*, Oxford University Press, Oxford, 1998.

Marwick, A., *Total War and Social Change*, Macmillan, London, 1998.

Mass Observation, *Home Propaganda*, Advertising Service Guild, London, 1941.

Mass Observation, *People in Production*, John Murray, London, 1942.

Matthews, W.R., *St Paul's Cathedral in Wartime*, Hutchinson, London, 1946.

Mayhew, P. (ed.), *One Family's War*, Hutchinson, london, 1985.

Mee, A., *Nineteen-Forty: Our Finest Hour*, Hodder and Stoughton, London, 1941.

Meisel, J.S., 'Air raid shelter policy', *Twentieth Century British History*, Vol 5, No 1, 1994.

Middlemas, K., Power, *Competition and the State*, Macmillan, London, 1986.

Middleton, D., *The Sky Suspended: The Battle of Britain*, Secker & Waburg, London, 1960.

'Miles' (Neil Bell), *The Gas War of 1940*, Scolartis, London, 1931.

Miles, P. and Smith, M., *Cinema, Literature and Society*, Croom Helm, London, 1987.

Milward, A., *War, Economy and Society, 1939–1945*, Allen Lane, London, 1977.

Milward, A., *The Reconstruction of Western Europe*, University of California Press, Berkeley, 1984.

Mommsen, W.J. (ed.), *The Emergence of the Welfare State*, Croom Helm, London, 1981.

Moon, H., *The Invasion of the United Kingdom*, Ph.D. Thesis, University of London, 1968.

Morgan, D. and Evans, M., *The Battle for Britain*, Routledge, London, 1993.

Morgan, K.O., *Rebirth of a Nation: Wales 1880–1980*, Oxford University Press, Oxford, 1981.

Morgan, K.O., *Labour in Power*, Oxford University Press, Oxford, 1984.

Morgan, K.O., *The People's Peace*, Oxford University Press, Oxford, 1990.

Mowat, C.L., *Britain Between the Wars*, Methuen, London, 1955.

Muggeridge, M., *The Thirties: 1930–1940 in Britain*, Weidenfeld & Nicolson, 1940.

Murrow, E., *This is London*, Cassell, London, 1941.

NFWI, *Town Children Through Country Eyes*, NFWI, Dorking, 1940.

Nairn, T., *The Break-Up of Britain*, New Left Books, London, 1977.

Nicholas, H.G., *The British General Election of 1950*, Macmillan, London, 1951.

Nicholas, S., '"Sly demagogues" . . .', *20th Century British History*, 1995, pp. 247–66.

Nicholas, S., *The Echo of War*, Manchester University Press, Manchester, 1996.

Nicolson, N., Harold Nicolson, *Diaries and Letters*, Vol 2, Atheneum, New York, 1967.

Nixon, B., *Raiders Overhead*, Lindsay Drummond, London, 1943.

Noakes, J. (ed.), *The Civilian in War*, Exeter University Press, Exeter, 1992.

Noakes, L., *War and the British*, Taurus, London, 1998.

O'Brien, T.H., *Civil Defence*, HMSO, London, 1950.

Orwell, G., *Keep the Aspidistra Flying*, Gollancz, London, 1936, repr. Penguin, 1962.

Orwell, G., *Homage to Catalonia*, Gollancz, London, 1938, repr. Penguin, 1980.

Orwell, S. and Angus, I. (eds), *Collected Essays, Journalism and Letters of George Orwell, 4 vols*, Penguin, Harmondsworth, 1970.

Padley, R. and Cole, M. (eds), *Evacuation Survey*, Routledge, London, 1940.

Paris, M., *From the Wright Brothers to Top Gun*, Manchester University Press, Manchester, 1995.

Parker, H.M.D., *Manpower*, HMSO, London, 1957.

Parker, R., *Chamberlain and Appeasement*, Macmillan, London, 1993.

Pelling, H., *America and the British Left*, A & C Black, London, 1956.

Pelling, H., *Britain and the Second World War*, Fontana, London, 1970.

Ponting, C., *1940: Myth and Reality*, Hamish Hamilton, London, 1990.

Postan, M.M., *British War Production*, HMSO, London, 1952.

Priestley, J.B., *English Journey*, Heinemann, London, 1934.

Priestley, J.B., *Postscripts*, Heinemann, London, 1940.

Prittie,T., *Konrad Adenauer*, T. Stacey, London, 1972.

Rabinow, P., *The Foucault Reader*, Penguin, Harmondsworth, 1991.

Radford, F.H., *Fetch the Engine*, Fire Brigades Union, London, 1951.

Ransome, P., *Antonio Gramsci*, Harvester, Brighton, 1992.

Reynolds, D., '1940: fulcrum of the 20th century?', *International Affairs*, Vol 66, 1990, pp. 325–50.

Reynolds, D., *Britannia Overruled*, Longman, London, 1991.

Reynolds, Q., *Britain Can Take It: The Book of the Film*, John Murray, London, 1941.

Reynolds, Q., *Only the Stars are Neutral*, Cassell, London, 1942.

Reynolds, Q., *By Quentin Reynolds*, Heinemann, London, 1964.

Richards, J.M., *Bombed Buildings of Britain*, Architectural Press, London, 1947.

Richards, J., *Films and British National Identity*, Manchester University Press, Manchester, 1997.

Ridell, P., *The Thatcher Government*, M. Robertson, Oxford, 1983.

Robbins, K.G., *Churchill*, Longman, London, 1992.

Robbins, K.G., *The Eclipse of a Great Power*, Longman, London, 1994.

Robbins, T., *Skinny Legs and All*, Bantam, New York, 1990.

Robins, L.J., *The Reluctant Party: Labour and the EEC*, Hesketh, Ormskirk, 1979.

Rollo, P.J.V., *Britain and the Briand Plan*, Keele University Press, Keele, 1972.

Rosenstone, R., *Revisioning History*, Princeton University Press, Princeton NJ, 1995.

Rosenstone, R., *Visions of the Past*, Harvard University Press, Cambridge, MA, 1995.

Rowlinson, F., *Contribution to Victory*, Metropolitan Vickers, Manchester, 1947.

Sampson, A., *The New Anatomy of Britain*, Stein & Day, New York, 1971.

Samuel, R. (ed.), *Patriotism*, 3 vols, Routledge, London, 1989.

Samuel, S., 'The Left Book Club', *Journal of Contemporary History*, Vol 1, No 2, 1966.

Sansom, W., *Westminster at War*, Faber, London, 1947.

Sayers, R.S., *Financial Policy*, HMSO and Longmans, London, 1956.

Scott, J.D. and Hughes, R., *The Administration of War Production*, HMSO, London, 1955.

Segal, C.S., *Backward Children in the Making*, Muller, London, 1949.

Shakespeare, G., *Let Candles be Brought In*, Macdonald, London, 1949.

Shanks, E., *People of the Ruins*, Stokes, New York, 1920.

Sheffield Telegraph and Star, *Sheffield at War*, Sheffield, 1948.

Shindler, C., *Hollywood Goes to War*, Routledge & Kegan Paul, London, 1979.

Shipley, Revd S.P., *Bristol Siren Nights*, Rankin, Bristol, 1943.

Shlaim, A., *Britain and the Origins of European Unity*, University of Reading, Reading 1978.

Smith, H.L. (ed.), *War and Social Change*, Manchester University Press, Manchester, 1986.

Smith, M., 'A matter of faith', *Journal of the RUSI*, 1976, pp. 68–73.

Smith, M., *British Air Strategy between the Wars*, Clarendon, Oxford, 1984.

Smith, M., *British Politics, Society and the State*, Macmillan, Basingstoke, 1990.

Smith, M., *Democracy in a Depression*, University of Wales Press, Cardiff, 1998.

Sperber, A.M., *Murrow: His Life and Times*, Michael Joseph, London, 1987.

Stedman, H.W., *Battle of the Flames*, Harrolds, London, 1942.

Stevenson, J., *British Society, 1914–45*, Penguin, London, 1984.

Stevenson, J and Cook, C., *The Slump*, Cape, London, 1977.

Strachey, J., *A Programme for Progress*, Gollancz, London, 1940.

Strachey, J., *A Faith to Fight For*, Gollancz, London, 1941.

Strachey, J., *Post D*, Gollancz, London, 1941.

Street, A.G., *From Dusk till Dawn*, Blandford, London, 1947.

Street, S., *British National Cinema*, Routledge, London, 1997.

Sussex. E., *The Rise and Fall of Documentary*, University of California Press, Berkeley, 1975.

Taylor, A.J.P., *English History, 1914–45*, Oxford University Press, Oxford, 1965.

Taylor, A.J.P., *Churchill: Four Faces and the Man*, Penguin, Harmondsworth, 1973.

Taylor, J.R., *A Dream of England*, Manchester University Press, Manchester, 1994.

Taylor, P., *The Limits of European Integration*, Croom Helm, London, 1983.

Taylor, T., *The Breaking Wave*, Weidenfeld & Nicolson, London, 1967.

Templewood, Viscount (Sir Samuel Hoare), *Nine Troubled Years*, London, 1954.

Thomas, P. (ed.), *Mass Observation in World War II*, University of Sussex, Brighton, 1988.

Thompson, L., *1940: Year of Legend and History*, Collins, London, 1966.

Thoms, D.C., *War, Industry and Society: The Midlands, 1939–45*, Routledge, London, 1989.

Tiquet, S., *It Happened Here*, Wanstead and Woodford Borough Council, 1947.

Tiratsoo, N. (ed.), *The Attlee Years*, Pinter, London, 1991.

Titmuss, R., *Problems of Social Policy*, HMSO, London, 1950.

Tracey, H., *Trade Unions Fight – For What?*, Routledge, London, 1940.

Trevor Roper, H. (ed.), *Hitler's War Directives*, Pan, London, 1966.

Turner, E.S., *The Phoney War on the Home Front*, Michael Joseph, London, 1951.

Twyford, H.P., *It Came to Our Door*, Underhill, Plymouth, 1946.

Underdown, T.H.J., *Bristol Under Blitz*, Arrowsmith, Bristol, 1942.

Walmsley, L., *Fishermen at War*, Collins, London, 1941.

Watt, H., *Don't Look at the Camera*, Elek, London, 1974.

Webb, M., *Britain's Industrial Front*, Odhams, London, 1943.

Webster, C., *The Health Services Since the War*, Vol 1, HMSO, London, 1988.

Wells, H.G., *The New World Order*, Secker & Warburg, London, 1940.

Wheeler Bennett, J., *John Anderson, First Viscount Waverley*, Macmillan, London, 1962.

Wheeler, H., *Huddersfield at War*, Alan Sutton, Bath, 1992.

Williams, F., *Ernest Bevin*, Hutchinson, London, 1952.

Williams, F., *A Prime Minister Remembers*, Heinemann, London, 1961.

Williams, G., *Women and Work*, Nicholson & Watson, London, 1945.

Williams, G. A., *When was Wales?*, Penguin, Harmondsworth, 1985.

Winter, J. (ed.), *War And Economic Development*, Cambridge University Press, Cambridge, 1975.

Wintringham, T., *New Ways of War*, Penguin Special, London, 1940.

Women's Group on Public Welfare, *Our Towns*, Oxford University Press, Oxford, 1943.

Wood, D. and Dempster, D., *The Narrow Margin*, Hutchinson, London, 1961.

Woon, B., *Hell Came to London*, Peter Davies, London, 1941.

Wright, G., *The Ordeal of Total War*, New York, Harper & Row, 1968.

Wright, P., *On Living in an Old Country*, Verso, London, 1985.

Wright, R., *Dowding and the Battle of Britain*, Penguin, London 1969.

Wrigley, G. (ed.), *A History of British Industrial Relations*, Edward Elgar, Cheltenham, 1996.

Young, H., *One of Us: A Biography of Margaret Thatcher*, Pan Macmillan, London, 1990.

Young, J.W., *Britain, France and the Unity of Europe*, Leicester University Press, Leicester, 1984.

Young, J.W., *Britain and European Unity 1945–92*, Macmillan, London, 1993.

Young, K., *Churchill and Beaverbrook*, Eyre & Spottiswoode, London, 1966.

Young, S., *Terms of Entry*, Heinemann, London, 1973.

Ziegler, P., *London at War, 1939–45*, Alfred Knopf, New York, 1995

Index